SELECTED POEMS

OF

CHRISTINA ROSSETTI

SELECTED POEMS

OF

CHRISTINA ROSSETTI

EDITED AND WITH AN INTRODUCTION BY

MARYA ZATURENSKA

THE MACMILLAN COMPANY

COLLIER-MACMILLAN LTD.

LONDON

The Macmillan Company
866 Third Avenue, New York, N.Y. 10022
Collier-Macmillan Canada Ltd., Toronto, Ontario

Printed in the United States of America

For Patrick and Justina Gregory

CONTENTS

SELECTED POEMS

OF

CHRISTINA
ROSSETTI

INTRODUCTION

The Passionate Austerity of Christina Rossetti

"IT is said that in Great Britain thousands of years ago when an unknown people were celebrating the summer solstice in a circle of upright stones . . . a religious chant could be heard through the night, like far-off bells; the Sacred Swans were singing." So Dominique Aury, the French critic, ends an essay on Chrétien de Troyes, the poet of Celtic Brittany. The music of the Sacred Swans is heard too when song and indefinable magic rise from some pure source of lyric poetry. How else can one describe it but as *magic*, for the enchantment is inexplicable. One feels it and is grateful.

The women who have written lyric poetry of great merit in English are few. And it is a matter of common knowledge that, in the arts and sciences, women have not taken a first place. Perhaps some ardent feminist may make a study of this one day and come up with a sympathetic answer. One can only say that, while talent is plentiful, genius, after all, is always startling and rare. To the list of women who have achieved real distinction in poetry I should like to add the name of Christina Rossetti. If she and other women lyric poets of great merit do

3

not approach the genius of Shakespeare, Dante, Dryden, Goethe, or Wordsworth, they nevertheless have an authentic beauty of their own. Christina Rossetti does not often have the wild facility too frequently found in the lesser women poets and certainly has made no attempt to ape masculine attitudes; she is truly herself.

Though the Rossetti family did have some English blood, they were not proper Victorians—but Christina and her mother attempted to be as English as possible. Even in their passionate and truly devout adherence to the Anglican Church there was a touch of Italian mystical fervor. But Christina, quiet, reserved, and noted for her beautiful low voice, was always somewhat of an exotic in English life and letters. There is a subtle Italian music in her poetry. She brought an Italianate softness and grace to the English lyric.

The Rossettis originated in a little town in the Abruzzi called Vasto—once a part of the old kingdom of Naples. It is a forgotten place situated high above the Adriatic. To this day it has little attraction for the tourist, except for its antiquity and sea-rimmed walls. Most natives are olive growers and fishermen.

Gabriele Rossetti, the father of Christina and Dante Gabriel, is Vasto's own poet. The main square of the town is named after him. The birthplace of Gabriele has been bought by the town and is now a Rossetti museum. Though he is not listed among Italy's greatest poets today, Gabriele Rossetti is at least honored in his own country. Born in 1783, the son of a blacksmith, he was—as was all Europe—carried away by the Romantic Movement that hand in hand with revolution changed the face of Europe and Italy as well. He was all fire, enthusiasm, and dramatic temperament. One recognizes that like many an inadequate poet he put more into his personality than into his poetry. After many adventures, he had to fly from the wrath of the Bourbons and came to England, where he found refuge and an Italian wife who was half-English on her mother's side. In England his charming, colorful personality found him friends, patrons, and a group of Italian exiles who looked to him as a leader in the fight that was to result in Italian liberation. They seemed to spend their lives plotting revolution, declaiming and writing poetry (too grandiose and eloquent to be quite convincing), and studying, talking, and writing about Dante, who was just coming into vogue in England. The Rossettis always had a strange, magnetic force and what the progressive schools used to call "leadership capacity." Dante Gabriel Rossetti, poet and artist, was his father's son and inherited many of his characteristics—the moments of coarseness, the exquisite refinement, the fine sensibility, the mysticism that led him by temperament to develop a hate-love toward the Catholic faith and to fill his rich subaqueous music, his overornamented, glowing paintings with its mysteries and symbols. Dante Gabriel's vigorous magnetism influenced everyone he met, and if he is not technically the father of the Pre-Raphaelite movement, what of it? The others now seem dim and shadowy. When one thinks of the Pre-Raphaelites, unless one excepts William Morris, it is usually Dante Gabriel who first comes to mind. And yet Christina was not quite a Pre-Raphaelite; her magic *is* her own and, ultimately, unclassifiable.

Christina, born in 1830, was always her mother's daughter—a Polidori more than a Rossetti. The Polidori were cultivated Florentines—Tuscans who were blue-eyed, overrefined, and almost overcultivated. The Polidoris' contribution to Christina's poetry and temperament have been neglected. From them she inherited her delicate classic features, hazel eyes, lovely voice, and beautiful manners. The Polidoris were Italians of Greek descent and were moderately prosperous. They, too, had fled to England during the revolutionary turmoils in Italy. Like the Rossettis, and the descendants of the Blacksmith of Vasto, the Polidoris were bursting with literary ambitions even before the birth of Gabriel or Christina and had a small place in literary history. The Polidori grandfather of the Rossettis had been private secretary to Count Alfieri, the forerunner of the Italian Romantic Movement whose poems and dramas transformed Italian literature. With Count Alfieri, Gaetano Polidori had visited France and witnessed the fall of the Bastille. After seing Alfieri through many amorous adventures (Alfieri later eloped with the wife of "Bonnie Prince Charlie"), Polidori decided to settle in England after Alfieri left England in a wave of scandal after fighting a duel with an English nobleman whose wife he had seduced. Polidori on the whole seemed prim and proper and domestic by nature and no doubt he was glad when he became an English subject and his Alfieri days were over. It was before Victoria's Prince Consort taught English intellectuals to popularize Goethe at the expense of Dante, but Italian was still a fashionable language. Polidori taught Italian literature, wrote Italian grammars, and took an English bride, Anna Maria Pearce, a governess who came from a stout Tory family which could not understand why their daughter married an Italian. Polidori prospered enough to buy a small house in the country. Three Polidori daughters earned their way as governesses, like true Brontë heroines. There were also three Polidori uncles, one of whom, John Polidori was an intimate and traveling physician of Lord Byron.

Byron found him amusing, interesting, and exasperating all at once and could never understand his own fondness for that impossible character. Polidori was with Byron in Switzerland when the Shelleys joined them. He disliked Shelley at once and thought he was what is now called a psychopathic liar. He was with Byron and the Shelleys when they sat around the fire one evening and told ghost stories that ultimately resulted in Mary Shelley writing *Frankenstein*. Polidori was inspired too. He wrote a novel called *The Vampyre* full of Gothic horrors that he published anonymously, allowing the publisher's publicity to hint that the book was by Lord Byron. The press references to this became a nuisance to Byron, who had never heard of the book or read it.

Byron was tiring of Polidori, who had become boring, envious of Byron, jealous of Byron's friendship for Shelley. Polidori began to talk of "spiritual servitude." His attitude to Byron was full of passionate love, passionate hate, and a complete misunderstanding of Byron's character. What could Byron do, Polidori asked, that was beyond *his* own abilities? "Why, since you force me to say," answered Byron, "I can snuff out that candle with a pistol shot at a distance of twenty paces—and I can swim across that river—and I have written a poem of which fourteen thousand copies were sold in one day." This remark had its effect. Polidori rushed to his room and, after writing a farewell note to Byron, attempted suicide. Byron tapped on the door, extended his hand in kindliness, and prevented this suicide attempt. Although His Lordship was no doubt happy to see Polidori go, some time later, when Byron heard that Polidori had at last successfully committed suicide (he seemed to have killed himself because of an overdose of Byronism), it was noted that he seemed much affected. Byron said he had dreamed of Polidori before his death and had felt that Polidori was telling him that something unhappy was about to happen.

Christina and her mother rarely mentioned this most improper relative, but his portrait always hung unnoticed in some obscure corner of their home. Years later Christina, ill and morbidly obsessed with the idea of an angry God who could not tolerate the awful sin of suicide, hung this portrait in her own room. Did she keep it there to meditate on sin and family madness or out of a secret sympathy? As the old saying goes, her secret was always her own. We do know that at one time her brother Dante Gabriel attempted suicide. Dante Gabriel's wife "The Blessed Damosel" of his pictures was certainly a suicide (though an attempt was made to hide the fact). And Christina had always disliked "The Blessed Damosel"!

With a family so given up to literature on both sides, it was time for the Rossetti-Polidori clan to produce writers of acknowledged merit. Suddenly the suppressed and the half-suppressed dreams of the two families became a reality with Christina and her brother Dante Gabriel, both so rare and so rich in talent and feeling; the half-pagan Dante Gabriel with his love of Roman Catholic ritual, and the intense, mystical Christina, who, in spite of her Latin soul and temperament, thought of herself as very English and a devout Anglican. But an Italian fervor firmly held within a strict Church of England orthodoxy gave her devotional verse its exotic flavor and also resulted in some of the most beautiful love poems in the English language—passionate in their feeling, delicate in their undercurrent of sensuality, and very Latin in their often erotic mysticism. No other woman has written poems of such sensuous beauty as she when she turned from religion and wrote her love poems. They seem to be drawn from a single source of natural inspiration and of divided sensibilities.

> But bring me poppies brimmed with sleepy death
> And ivy choking what it garlandeth
> And primroses that open to the moon.

Or the much anthologized "A Birthday," one of the truest examples of the pure lyric in English.

> Raise me a dais of silk and down;
>   Hang it with vair and purple dyes;
> Carve it in doves and pomegranates,
>   And peacocks with a hundred eyes;
> Work it in gold and silver grapes,
>   In leaves and silver fleur-de-lys;
> Because the birthday of my life
>   Is come, my love is come to me.

This and other poems like the delightful genre picture "An Apple Gathering" are part of the singing poems of her youth before poverty, continual bad health, and frustration had taken its toll, while in the last sonnet of her "Monna Innominata" series she epitomized the later tone of her love poems. This sonnet-sequence, one of the finest in the language, is a veritable song book of unhappy love. In this sequence she sums up this side of her life once and for all. Here again we feel an undercurrent of nervous strength and hear that piercing Italian music running through a low-keyed English tone of understatement.

Youth gone, and beauty gone, if ever there
    Dwelt beauty in so poor a face as this;
    Youth gone and beauty, what remains of bliss?
I will not bind fresh roses in my hair,
To shame a cheek at best but little fair,—
    Leave youth his roses, who can bear a thorn,—
I will not seek for blossoms anywhere,
    Except such common flowers as blow with corn.
Youth gone, and beauty gone, what doth remain?
    The longing of a heart pent up forlorn,
      A silent heart whose silence loves and longs;
      The silence of a heart which sang its songs
    While youth and beauty made a summer morn,
Silence of love that cannot sing again.

We have an early and attractive picture of Christina as a young girl in her teens as she was seen by William Bell Scott, a friend of Dante Gabriel Rossetti's. Scott had shown promise as a painter and poet in his youth and had later, when that promise had evaporated, published memoirs in which envy, bad temper, and frustration dominated. He turned against the Rossettis and other members of the Pre-Raphaelites who had achieved the fame which is not always success but seems so to one like Scott, who basked in the admiration and patronage of many rich, undiscriminating, elderly women. But he was young then, and had received a letter of praise from Dante Gabriel who was the rising star of the younger generation. Scott was quick to describe what he saw, and he gave us a clear picture of the Rossetti family and the interior of their shabby but fascinating household. Entering the small parlor, which was also a dining room, Scott was asked to wait for a while till Dante Gabriel came down from his upstairs study. Old Gabriele greeted Scott with politeness and engaged him in conversation. He was sitting in a large armchair near a window with an enormous manuscript in his hand. No doubt it was his extensive study of Dante. Year after year old Gabriele, who had named his eldest son after Dante, worked on this evergrowing manuscript in which he traced certain secret Freemasonry symbols hidden in the text of the *Divine Comedy*. There was evidence, he thought, to prove that Dante was a Freemason before his day, and that a secret, a great message, could be deciphered from it all, once one had found the key. He *had* found the key and soon he would unravel the great secret. Old Gabriele was growing blind but his work kept him happy. A few rich patrons and his younger son William Michael, who had begun his career as a civil servant in Somerset House, kept the family in very moderate comfort.

The light of day was slowly diminishing, but in the growing twilight Scott kept watching the most interesting person (to him!) in the room. This was a slight, graceful girl of about seventeen who stood before a high, narrow reading desk writing. So seriously was she absorbed that she hardly looked up at first to see the visitor. He noticed the simple costume that gave her an air of quiet elegance, her pure classic profile, and her dark smooth hair. Introduced to her, he was struck by her unusual hazel eyes that contrasted with her dark hair. She said a few polite words to the visitor and then made a most formal and graceful curtsey and retired. Her grace and classic beauty at this period have been remarked on by more than William Bell Scott, and there are portraits, photographs, and testimonials to prove this. But already the inflexible spirit that was to guide her life, her poetry, and her religion, had entered. Later she became more and more careless of her charm, her grace, and her beauty. She felt it might distract her from God—might distract her from poetry. It is possible that like Emily Dickinson, her very close contemporary, she was protecting her Muse, her gift against even greater handicaps than the Swan of Amherst, Massachusetts knew. And her suitors were all decidedly ineligible!

The Anglican Church also held her with a fervor that her Roman Catholic ancestors might not have thought strange but which often embarrassed her fellow Anglicans who dismissed the high church enthusiasms of the Oxford movement as "High Jinks." The Anglican Church, though it has its saints and martyrs, does not canonize them. A study of Christina's few devotional works in prose prove beautiful enough to give her a place among the true Anglican mystics. While her devotional prose works are hardly known, a few of her poems have entered the hymn books and are sung. The great body of her devotional poems place her among the small group of poets who have made their religious verse into something as great as their theme, something more than a spiritual exercise.

When William Bell Scott first met young Christina, she had already been writing her poems; in fact she could never remember a time when she had not been writing poems. She had a natural and fine gift for exquisite music as artfully simple as a song by Mozart. It was a gift she kept all her life. Her ear, almost flawless, was one of the most musical in the English language. Even her devotional poems move with a melody that is sometimes piercing, sometimes almost majestic.

One would like to quote one of her devotional masterpieces, "Sleep at Sea," but it cannot be quoted in excerpts. It is too strongly integrated. George Saintsbury, an English critic worth taking seriously, speaks of it as one of the great devotional poems in the language. Its immediate imagery catches the very movement of the sea as seen through a thick atmosphere of fog. The vision of the dead arising from their ocean graves and flitting from mast to mast in aimless terror is magnificent. It also reveals Christina in her Somber Vision of Eternity—a steady movement toward suffering and terror before the goal of eternal bliss and endless peace is reached. One would also like to quote one strangely beautiful poem after another to prove her remarkable ear, her technical skill, and her visionary penetration into the mysteries of life and death. Take, for instance, this Easter Tuesday poem with its hesitant endings.

'Together with my dead body shall they arise.'
Shall my dead body arise? then amen and yea
On track of a home beyond the uttermost skies
Together with my dead body shall they.

We know the way: thank God Who hath showed us the way!
Jesus Christ our Way to beautiful Paradise,
Jesus Christ the Same for ever, the Same to-day.

Five Virgins replenish with oil their lamps, being wise,
Five Virgins awaiting the Bridegroom watch and pray:
And if I one day spring from my grave to the prize,
Together with my dead body shall they.

Where can we hear lovelier music than in the better-known love
poem "Echo," where the soft closing and shutting of a door
seems to move to a dreamlike music?

O dream too sweet, too sweet, too bitter sweet,
Whose wakening should have been in Paradise
Where souls brimful of love abide and meet;
Where thirsting longing eyes
Watch the slow door
That opening, letting in, lets out no more

*   *   *

Speak low, lean low,
As long ago my love, how long ago.

Christina Rossetti's devotional poems require special study:
they are among the few religious poems in English that can be
read with pleasure by those who do not share her views. A
glance over the section in this volume which includes her religious verse will prove my point. Her feeling of devotion is not
facile, her faith is never comfortable or assured. There are
moments when her intensity reminds us of Gerard Hopkins when
he wrote of the Terrible Crystal and his moments of doubt and

despair. Profound faith, in its best sense, is a gift of grace to the mystic or inspired poet. Christina is one of the few who had been granted this gift.

'I have not sought Thee, I have not found Thee,
    I have not thirsted for Thee:
And now cold billows of death surround me,
Buffeting billows of death astound me,—
    Wilt Thou look upon, wilt Thou see
    Thy perishing Me?'

'Yea, I have sought thee, yea I have found thee,
    Yea, I have thirsted for thee,
Yea, long ago with love's bands I bound thee
Now the Everlasting Arms surround thee,—
    Through death's darkness I look and see
    And clasp thee to Me.'

One is tempted to quote a portion of her "Good Friday" poem if only to display her power to pierce the heart.

Not so those women loved
    Who with exceeding grief lamented Thee;
    Not so fallen Peter weeping bitterly;
Not so the thief was moved;

Not so the Sun and Moon
    Which hid their faces in a starless sky,
A horror of great darkness at broad noon—
    I, only I.

Yet give not o'er,
    But seek Thy sheep, true Shepherd of the flock;
Greater than Moses, turn and look once more
    And smite a rock.

But she could also write in one of her last poems,

13

Heaven overarches earth and sea,
Earth-sadness and sea-bitterness.
Heaven overarches you and me:
A little while and we shall be—
Please God—where there is no more sea
Nor barren wilderness.

An aerial music akin to Shelley's skylark sounds through many of her shorter lyrics of love, human destiny, and her limited moments of passionate living. The passion is often concentrated in narrow, tight forms; but being an artist, the feeling is purely and deeply contained within the natural ease and the perfection of her form. What can be more graceful, more classical in the Renaissance sense than the poem that opens this volume— "Venus's Looking-Glass"? In reading this poem one is somehow reminded of another small masterpiece of English verse, Sir Walter Raleigh's sonnet beginning "Methought I saw the grave where Laura lay."* Indeed many of her love lyrics do give the impression that her kinship was very often with the Elizabethan lyricists and occasionally with the Cavalier poets rather than with the Victorians. There *was* often something oddly un-Victorian in her diction, her feeling, and her art. This no doubt would have surprised Christina, who had a portrait of the young Queen Victoria in her drawing room. Her first volume, *Goblin Market*, published in 1862, contains what many consider her masterpiece; the title poem was certainly the only successful long poem she ever wrote. Set in a lush Pre-Raphaelite landscape (a boon for popular illustrators), it has a rather repellent beauty and a fascinating atmosphere that is both evil and supernatural. It contains all the suppressed innocent sensuality disguised as something else which was not uncommon in Victorian art and life. Christina probably intended little more than an allegory ending with a surprise tribute to her equally devout sister Maria. But it became something more—a strange, macabre little master-

* "The Faery Queen," in which Raleigh invokes the Spirit of Petrarch.

14

piece—a real work of art. It contains her love for small animals, her obsession with the problems of evil, her close ties with her sister Maria and her mother. Who can forget her picture of the Goblin Men who try to buy her sister's soul with their dazzling fruit?

> The whisk-tailed merchant bade her taste
> In tones as soft as honey,
> The cat-faced purr'd
> The rat-faced spoke a word
> Of welcome and the snail-faced even was heard;
> One parrot-voiced and jolly
> Cried "Pretty Goblin" still for "Pretty Polly";—
> One whistled like a bird.

Christina Rossetti was never a bookish woman and was not interested enough in the fashions of her day to admire George Sand or George Eliot. But she read the then almost unread Turgenieff when he first appeared in English translation. We know she was much impressed by the posthumous volume of Emily Dickinson's verse that was sent to her by an American friend (though rather disturbed by her technique). She knew George Herbert, and Vaughan and Southwell. It is doubtful if she would have liked Donne's poetry, though she read his sermons and Jeremy Taylor's "Holy Living and Holy Dying."

Slowly her fame increased through her discovery by younger critics and through the loyal, almost passionate, support of Swinburne, whose work *she* did not admire. When John Addington Symonds, Arthur Symons, Lionel Johnson, and Oscar Wilde began to praise her, Robert Browning became annoyed, especially as she was often favorably compared to his adored Elizabeth. Christina had to send him a long, humble letter so full of admiration for Elizabeth Browning that he was mollified and came to tea with Christina and her mother. But he always retained his suspicions of all the Pre-Raphaelites.

In later years, Christina discovered the poems of Canon Dixon, friend of Gerard Hopkins. A favorite novelist was Mrs. Gaskell. She disliked and avoided technical discussions on poetry. When asked to write a volume in a publisher's series of Eminent Women, she could only think of Mrs. Radcliffe, one of the forerunners of the Gothic novel whose *Mysteries of Udolpho* she had much admired in her youth. Then she decided that she didn't like to read or write biographies—"It all ends in death"—and did not write the biography of Mrs. Radcliffe.

Christina Rossetti's surprising *Sing-Song* is one of the most delightful books of verses for children. It appeared in 1872 and was immediately recognized for the little classic it is. It is still read often and anthologized and it has been compared by Sir Sidney Colvin to Lear's *Nonsense Book* and Carroll's *Through the Looking-Glass*. It certainly bears signs of her reading of Blake, the poet much read and admired by the Pre-Raphaelites. In fact one can almost call him their discovery, as any literary historian can prove.

In editing this book I have tried to include a generous portion of Christina Rossetti's work—a difficult job, for her level is always high, and, like many of the great Victorian poets, she wrote too much. But indeed she was of that rare species, the Sacred Swans whose singing becomes more poignant as they approach the end. Unlike Emily Brontë, whose book of poems was left incomplete, Christina Rossetti did leave a full body of poems, and her place among English poets is unique. Dorothy Stuart, one of her admirers and biographers, summed up her quality.

Elizabeth Barrett Browning's imagination was like an impetuous flood, constantly breaking through dyke and dams, and so spreading itself into a chain of vast lagoons, shallows and . . . islands. And here lies the strongest contrasts between her and Christina Rossetti, whose mind having no such foaming onsets, no such tranquil expansions, carved out for itself, a deep though narrow channel and thrust its way ever darkening toward the unseen sea.

After her death in 1894, her work, with its unashamed femininity and avoidance of literary showmanship, received its share of male patronage. She was admired and esteemed, but her books sold badly at first and it was a long time before she secured an ever-widening public and fame. When Andrew Lang, one of the most influential critics of the day, wrote her obituary he said:

> There can be little doubt that we are now deprived of the greatest English poet of her sex which is made to inspire poetry rather than to create it.

This is indeed intolerable praise and it would have taken all of Christina's Christian humility to take. But she had always been true to her unique gift and her peculiar, individual vision. She has survived Andrew Lang, who was also a poet and she has a secure place among the true poets in the English language. As the modern English critic, Cyril Connolly, has said, "Literary history goes to prove that lyrical poetry is the medium which more than any other defies time." And Christina Rossetti is a lyric poet of a very high order.

MARYA ZATURENSKA

Palisades, New York

LOVE POEMS

Venus's Looking-Glass

I marked where lovely Venus and her court
    With song and dance and merry laugh went by;
    Weightless, their wingless feet seemed made to fly,
Bound from the ground, and in mid air to sport.
Left far behind I heard the dolphins snort,
    Tracking their goddess with a wistful eye,
    Around whose head white doves rose, wheeling high
Or low, and cooed after their tender sort.
All this I saw in Spring. Through summer heat
    I saw the lovely Queen of Love no more
    But when flushed Autumn through the woodlands went
I spied sweet Venus walk amid the wheat:
    Whom seeing, every harvester gave o'er
    His toil, and laught and hoped and was content.

The Hour and The Ghost

BRIDE

O Love, love, hold me fast,
He draws me away from thee;
I cannot stem the blast,
Nor the cold strong sea:
Far away a light shines
Beyond the hills and pines;
It is lit for me.

BRIDEGROOM

I have thee close, my dear,
No terror can come near;
Only far off the northern light shines clear.

GHOST

Come with me, fair and false,
To our home, come home.
It is my voice that calls:
Once thou wast not afraid
When I woo'd, and said,
'Come, our nest is newly made'—
Now cross the tossing foam.

BRIDE

Hold me one moment longer!
He taunts me with the past,

His clutch is waxing stronger;
Hold me fast, hold me fast.
He draws me from thy heart,
And I cannot withhold:
He bids my spirit depart
With him into the cold:—
Oh bitter vows of old!

BRIDEGROOM

Lean on me, hide thine eyes:
Only ourselves, earth and skies,
Are present here: be wise.

GHOST

Lean on me, come away,
I will guide and steady:
Come, for I will not stay:
Come, for house and bed are ready.
Ah sure bed and house,
For better and worse, for life and death,
Goal won with shortened breath!
Come, crown our vows.

BRIDE

One moment, one more word,
While my heart beats still,
While my breath is stirred
By my fainting will.
O friend, forsake me not,
Forget not as I forgot:
But keep thy heart for me,
Keep thy faith true and bright;
Through the lone cold winter night
Perhaps I may come to thee.

23

B R I D E G R O O M
Nay peace, my darling, peace:
Let these dreams and terrors cease:
Who spoke of death or change or aught but ease?

G H O S T
O fair frail sin,
O poor harvest gathered in!
Thou shalt visit him again
To watch his heart grow cold:
To know the gnawing pain
I knew of old;
To see one much more fair
Fill up the vacant chair,
Fill his heart, his children bear;
While thou and I together,
In the outcast weather,
Toss and howl and spin.

Song

When I am dead, my dearest,
    Sing no sad songs for me;
Plant thou no roses at my head,
    Nor shady cypress tree:
Be the green grass above me
    With showers and dewdrops wet:
And if thou wilt, remember,
    And if thou wilt, forget.

I shall not see the shadows,
    I shall not feel the rain;
I shall not hear the nightingale
    Sing on as if in pain:
And dreaming through the twilight
    That doth not rise nor set,
Haply I may remember,
    And haply may forget.

Dream-Love

Young Love lies sleeping
    In May-time of the year,
Among the lilies,
    Lapped in the tender light:
White lambs come grazing,
    White doves come building there;
And round about him
    The May-bushes are white.

Soft moss the pillow
    For oh a softer cheek;
Broad leaves cast shadow
    Upon the heavy eyes:
There winds and waters
    Grow lulled and scarcely speak;
There twilight lingers
    The longest in the skies.

Young Love lies dreaming;
    But who shall tell the dream?
A perfect sunlight
    On rustling forest tips;
Or perfect moonlight
    Upon a ripling stream;
Or perfect silence,
    Or song of cherished lips.

Burns odours round him
    To fill the drowsy air;
Weave silent dances
    Around him to and fro;
For oh in waking
    The sights are not so fair,
And song and silence
    Are not like these below.

Young Love lies dreaming
    Till summer days are gone,—
Dreaming and drowsing
    Away to perfect sleep:
He sees the beauty
    Sun hath not looked upon,
And tastes the fountain
    Unutterably deep.

Him perfect music
    Doth hush unto his rest,
And through the pauses
    The perfect silence calms:
Oh poor the voices
    Of earth from east to west,
And poor earth's stillness
    Between her stately palms!

Young Love lies drowsing
    Away to poppied death;
Cool shadows deepen
    Across the sleeping face:
So fails the summer
    With warm delicious breath;
And what hath autumn
    To give us in its place?

Draw close the curtains
      Of branchèd evergreen;
Change cannot touch them
      With fading fingers sere:
Here the first violets
      Perhaps will bud unseen,
And a dove, may be,
      Return to nestle here.

From "*Songs for Strangers and Pilgrims*"

'Doeth well . . . doeth better.'

My love whose heart is tender said to me,
　'A moon lacks light except her sun befriend her.
Let us keep tryst in heaven, dear Friend,' said she,
　My love whose heart is tender.

　From such a loftiness no words could bend her:
Yet still she spoke of 'us' and spoke as 'we,'
　Her hope substantial, while my hope grew slender.

Now keeps she tryst beyond earth's utmost sea,
　Wholly at rest, tho' storms should toss and rend her;
And still she keeps my heart and keeps its key,
　My love whose heart is tender.

After Death

The curtains were half drawn, the floor was swept
    And strewn with rushes, rosemary and may
    Lay thick upon the bed on which I lay,
Where through the lattice ivy-shadows crept.
He leaned above me, thinking that I slept
    And could not hear him; but I heard him say,
    'Poor child, poor child': and as he turned away
Came a deep silence, and I knew he wept.
He did not touch the shroud, or raise the fold
    That hid my face, or take my hand in his,
    Or ruffle the smooth pillows for my head:
He did not love me living; but once dead
    He pitied me; and very sweet it is
To know he still is warm though I am cold.

An End

Love, strong as Death, is dead.
Come, let us make his bed
Among the dying flowers:
A green turf at his head;
And a stone at his feet,
Whereon we may sit
In the quiet evening hours.

He was born in the spring,
And died before the harvesting:
On the last warm summer day
He left us; he would not stay
For autumn twilight cold and grey.
Sit we by his grave, and sing
He is gone away.

To few chords sad and low
Sing we so:
Be our eyes fixed on the grass
Shadow-veiled as the years pass,
While we think of all that was
In the long ago.

An Apple Gathering

I plucked pink blossoms from mine apple-tree
    And wore them all that evening in my hair:
Then in due season when I went to see
    I found no apples there.

With dangling basket all along the grass
    As I had come I went the self-same track:
My neighbours mocked me while they saw me pass
    So empty-handed back.

Lilian and Lilias smiled in trudging by,
    Their heaped-up basket teased me like a jeer;
Sweet-voiced they sang beneath the sunset sky,
    Their mother's home was near.

Plump Gertrude passed me with her basket full,
    A stronger hand than hers helped it along;
A voice talked with her through the shadows cool
    More sweet to me than song.

Ah Willie, Willie, was my love less worth
    Than apples with their green leaves piled above?
I counted rosiest apples on the earth
    Of far less worth than love.

So once it was with me you stooped to talk
    Laughing and listening in this very lane;

To think that by this way we used to walk
    We shall not walk again!

I let my neighbours pass me, ones and twos
    And groups; the latest said the night grew chill
And hastened: but I loitered; while the dews
    Fell fast I loitered still.

From "*The Convent Threshold*"

I tell you what I dreamed last night.
A spirit with transfigured face
Fire-footed clomb an infinite space.
I heard his hundred pinions clang,
Heaven-bells rejoicing rang and rang,
Heaven-air was thrilled with subtle scents,
Worlds spun upon their rushing cars:
He mounted shrieking 'Give me light!'
Still light was poured on him, more light;
Angels, Archangels he outstripped,
Exultant in exceeding might,
And trod the skirts of Cherubim.
Still 'Give me light,' he shrieked; and dipped
His thirsty face, and drank a sea,
Athirst with thirst it could not slake.
I saw him, drunk with knowledge, take
From aching brows the aureole crown—
His locks writhe like a cloven snake—
He left his throne to grovel down
And lick the dust of Seraph's feet:
For what is knowledge duly weighed?
Knowledge is strong, but love is sweet;
Yea all the progress he had made
Was but to learn that all is small
Save love, for love is all in all.

I tell you what I dreamed last night.
It was not dark, it was not light,
Cold dews had drenched my plenteous hair
Through clay; you came to seek me there,
And 'Do you dream of me?' you said.
My heart was dust that used to leap
To you; I answered half asleep:
'My pillow is damp, my sheets are red,
There's a leaden tester to my bed:
Find you a warmer playfellow,
A warmer pillow for your head,
A kinder love to love than mine.'
You wrung your hands: while I, like lead,
Crushed downwards through the sodden earth:
You smote your hands but not in mirth,
And reeled but were not drunk with wine.

A Pause

They made the chamber sweet with flowers and leaves,
    And the bed sweet with flowers on which I lay;
    While my soul, love-bound, loitered on its way.
I did not hear the birds about the eaves,
Nor hear the reapers talk among the sheaves:
    Only my soul kept watch from day to day,
    My thirsty soul kept watch for one away:—
Perhaps he loves, I thought, remembers, grieves.
At length there came the step upon the stair,
    Upon the lock the old familiar hand:
Then first my spirit seemed to scent the air
    Of Paradise; then first the tardy sand
Of time ran golden; and I felt my hair
    Put on a glory, and my soul expand.

Echo

Come to me in the silence of the night;
    Come in the speaking silence of a dream;
Come with soft rounded cheeks and eyes as bright
    As sunlight on a stream;
        Come back in tears,
O memory, hope, love of finished years.

O dream how sweet, too sweet, too bitter sweet,
    Whose wakening should have been in Paradise,
Where souls brimfull of love abide and meet;
    Where thirsting longing eyes
        Watch the slow door
That opening, letting in, lets out no more.

Yet come to me in dreams, that I may live
    My very life again though cold in death:
Come back to me in dreams, that I may give
    Pulse for pulse, breath for breath:
        Speak low, lean low,
As long ago, my love, how long ago.

Moonshine

Fair the sun riseth,
    Bright as bright can be,
Fair the sun shineth
    On a fair fair sea.

'Across the water
Wilt thou come with me,
Miles and long miles, love,
Over the salt sea?'

'If thou wilt hold me
Truly by the hand,
    I will go with thee
Over sea and sand.

'If thou wilt hold me
That I shall not fall,
    I will go with thee,
Love, in spite of all.'

Fair the moon riseth
On her heavenly way,
    Making the waters
Fairer than by day.

    A little vessel
Rocks upon the sea,

Where stands a maiden
Fair as fair can be.

Her smile rejoices
Though her mouth is mute:
She treads the vessel
With her little foot.

Truly he holds her
Faithful to his pledge,
Guiding the vessel
From the water's edge.

Fair the moon saileth
With her pale fair light,
Fair the girl gazeth
Out into the night.

Saith she, 'Like silver
Shines thy hair, not gold':
Saith she, 'I shiver
In thy steady hold.

'Love,' she saith weeping,
'Loose thy hold awhile;
My heart is freezing
In thy freezing smile.'

The moon is hidden
By a silver cloud,
Fair as a halo
Or a maiden's shroud.

No more beseeching,
Ever on they go:

39

The vessel rocketh
Softly to and fro:

And still he holds her
That she shall not fall,
Till pale mists whiten
Dimly over all.

Onward and onward,
Far across the sea:
Onward and onward,
Pale as pale can be:

Onward and onward,
Ever hand in hand,
From sun and moonlight
To another land.

Mirage

The hope I dreamed of was a dream,
        Was but a dream; and now I wake,
Exceeding comfortless, and worn, and old,
        For a dream's sake.

I hang my harp upon a tree,
        A weeping willow in a lake;
I hang my silenced harp there, wrung and snapt
        For a dream's sake.

Lie still, lie still, my breaking heart:
        My silent heart, lie still and break:
Life, and the world, and mine own self, are changed
        For a dream's sake.

Remember

Remember me when I am gone away,
    Gone far away into the silent land;
    When you can no more hold me by the hand,
Nor I half turn to go yet turning stay.
Remember me when no more day by day
    You tell me of our future that you plann'd:
    Only remember me; you understand
It will be late to counsel then or pray.
Yet if you should forget me for a while
    And afterwards remember, do not grieve:
    For if the darkness and corruption leave
    A vestige of the thoughts that once I had,
Better by far you should forget and smile
    Than that you should remember and be sad.

Love Lies Bleeding

Love, that is dead and buried, yesterday
    Out of his grave rose up before my face;
    No recognition in his look, no trace
Of memory in his eyes dust-dimmed and grey;
While I, remembering, found no word to say,
    But felt my quickened heart leap in its place;
    Caught afterglow thrown back from long-set days,
Caught echoes of all music past away.
Was this indeed to meet?—I mind me yet
    In youth we met when hope and love were quick,
        We parted with hope dead but love alive:
I mind me how we parted then heart-sick,
    Remembering, loving, hopeless, weak to strive:—
Was this to meet? Not so, we have not met.

A Birthday

My heart is like a singing bird
    Whose nest is in a watered shoot;
My heart is like an apple tree
    Whose boughs are bent with thickset fruit;
My heart is like a rainbow shell
    That paddles in a halcyon sea;
My heart is gladder than all these
    Because my love is come to me.

Raise me a dais of silk and down;
    Hang it with vair and purple dyes;
Carve it with doves and pomegranates,
    And peacocks with a hundred eyes;
Work it in gold and silver grapes,
    In leaves and silver fleurs-de-lys
Because the birthday of my life
    Is come, my love is come to me.

Monna Innominata

A SONNET OF SONNETS

1

'Lo di che han detto a' dolci amici addio.'—DANTE
'Amor, con quanto sforzo oggi mi vinci!'—PETRARCA

Come back to me, who wait and watch for you:—
    Or come not yet, for it is over then,
    And long it is before you come again,
So far between my pleasures are and few.
While, when you come not, what I do I do
    Thinking 'Now when he comes,' my sweetest 'when';
    For one man is my world of all the men
This wide world holds; O love, my world is you.
Howbeit, to meet you grows almost a pang
    Because the pang of parting comes so soon;
    My hope hangs waning, waxing, like a moon
    Between the heavenly days on which we meet:
Ah me, but where are now the songs I sang
    When life was sweet because you called them sweet?

2

'Era già l'ora che volge il desio.'—DANTE
'Ricorro al tempo ch'io vi vidi prima.'—PETRARCA

I wish I could remember that first day,
    First hour, first moment of your meeting me,
    If bright or dim the season, it might be

Summer or Winter for aught I can say;
So unrecorded did it slip away,
    So blind was I to see and to foresee,
    So dull to mark the budding of my tree
That would not blossom yet for many a May.
If only I could recollect it, such
    A day of days! I let it come and go
    As traceless as a thaw of bygone snow;
It seemed to mean so little, meant so much;
If only now I could recall that touch,
    First touch of hand in hand—Did one but know!

3

'*O ombre vane, fuor che ne l'aspetto!*'—DANTE
'*Immaginata guida la conduce.*'—PETRARCA

I dream of you, to wake: would that I might
    Dream of you and not wake but slumber on;
    Nor find with dreams the dear companion gone,
As, Summer ended, Summer birds take flight.
In happy dreams I hold you full in sight,
    I blush again who waking look so wan;
    Brighter than sunniest day that ever shone,
In happy dreams your smile makes day of night.
Thus only in a dream we are at one,
    Thus only in a dream we give and take
        The faith that maketh rich who take or give;
    If thus to sleep is sweeter than to wake,
        To die were surely sweeter than to live,
Though there be nothing new beneath the sun.

4

'Poca favilla gran fiamma seconda.'—DANTE
'Ogni altra cosa, ogni pensier va fore,
E sol ivi con voi rimansi amore.'—PETRARCA

I loved you first: but afterwards your love,
 Outsoaring mine, sang such a loftier song
As drowned the friendly cooings of my dove.
 Which owes the other most? My love was long,
 And yours one moment seemed to wax more strong;
I loved and guessed at you, you construed me
And loved me for what might or might not be—
 Nay, weights and measures do us both a wrong.
For verily love knows not 'mine' or 'thine';
 With separate 'I' and 'thou' free love has done,
  For one is both and both are one in love:
Rich love knows nought of 'thine that is not mine;'
  Both have the strength and both the length thereof,
Both of us, of the love which makes us one.

5

 'Amor che a nullo armato amar perdona.'—DANTE
 'Amor m'addusse in si gioiosa spene.'—PETRARCA

O my heart's heart, and you who are to me
 More than myself myself, God be with you,
 Keep you in strong obedience leal and true
To Him whose noble service setteth free;
Give you all good we see or can foresee,
 Make your joys many and your sorrows few,
 Bless you in what you bear and what you do,
Yea, perfect you as He would have you be.
So much for you; but what for me, dear friend?
 To love you without stint and all I can,
To-day, to-morrow, world without an end;

47

To love you much and yet to love you more,
As Jordan at his flood sweeps either shore;
Since woman is the helpmeet made for man.

6

'Or puoi la quantitate
Comprender de l'amor che a te mi scalda.'—DANTE
'Non vo'che da tal nodo amor mi scioglia.'—PETRARCA

Trust me, I have not earned your dear rebuke,—
I love, as you would have me, God the most;
Would lose not Him, but you, must one be lost,
Nor with Lot's wife cast back a faithless look,
Unready to forego what I forsook;
This say I, having counted up the cost,
This, though I be the feeblest of God's host,
The sorriest sheep Christ shepherds with His crook.
Yet while I love my God the most, I deem
That I can never love you over-much;
I love Him more, so let me love you too;
Yea, as I apprehend it, love is such
I cannot love you if I love not Him,
I cannot love Him if I love not you.

7

'Qui primavera sempre ed ogni frutto.'—DANTE
'Ragionando con meco ed io con lui.'—PETRARCA

'Love me, for I love you'—and answer me,
'Love me, for I love you': so shall we stand
As happy equals in the flowering land
Of love, that knows not a dividing sea.
Love builds the house on rock and not on sand,
Love laughs what while the winds rave desperately;
And who hath found love's citadel unmanned?

48

And who hath held in bonds love's liberty?—
My heart's a coward though my words are brave—
We meet so seldom, yet we surely part
So often; there's a problem for your art!
Still I find comfort in his Book who saith,
Though jealousy be cruel as the grave,
And death be strong, yet love is strong as death.

8

'Come dicesse a Dio, D'altro non calme.'—DANTE
'Spero trovar pietà non che perdono.'—PETRARCA

'I, if I perish, perish'—Esther spake:
And bride of life or death she made her fair
In all the lustre of her perfumed hair
And smiles that kindle longing but to slake.
She put on pomp of loveliness, to take
Her husband through his eyes at unaware;
She spread abroad her beauty for a snare,
Harmless as doves and subtle as a snake.
She trapped him with one mesh of silken hair,
She vanquished him by wisdom of her wit,
And built her people's house that it should stand:—
If I might take my life so in my hand,
And for my love to Love put up my prayer,
And for love's sake by Love be granted it.

9

'O dignitosa coscienza e netta!'—DANTE
'Spirito più acceso di virtuti ardenti.'—PETRARCA

Thinking of you, and all that was, and all
That might have been and now can never be,
I feel your honoured excellence, and see

49

Myself unworthy of the happier call:
For woe is me who walk so apt to fall,
   So apt to shrink afraid, so apt to flee,
   Apt to lie down and die (ah woe is me!)
Faithless and hopeless turning to the wall.
And yet not hopeless quite nor faithless quite,
Because not loveless; love may toil all night,
But take at morning; wrestle till the break
   Of day, but then wield power with God and man: —
   So take I heart of grace as best I can,
Ready to spend and be spent for your sake.

10

'Con miglior corso e con migliore stella.'—DANTE
'La vita fugge e non s'arresta un' ora.'—PETRARCA

Time flies, hope flags, life plies a wearied wing;
   Death following hard on life gains ground apace;
   Faith runs with each and rears an eager face,
Outruns the rest, makes light of everything,
Spurns earth, and still finds breath to pray and sing;
   While love ahead of all uplifts his praise,
   Still asks for grace and still give thanks for grace,
Content with all day brings and night will bring.
Life wanes; and when love folds his wings above
   Tired hope, and less we feel his conscious pulse,
      Let us go fall asleep, dear friend, in peace:
      A little while, and age and sorrow cease;
   A little while, and life reborn annuls
Loss and decay and death, and all is love.

11

'Vien dietro a me a lascia dir le genti.'—DANTE
'Contando i casi della vita nostra.'—PETRARCA

Many in aftertimes will say of you
    'He loved her'—while of me what will they say?
    Not that I loved you more than just in play,
For fashion's sake as idle women do.
Even let them prate; who know not what we knew
    Of love and parting in exceeding pain,
    Of parting hopeless here to meet again,
Hopeless on earth, and heaven is out of view.
But by my heart of love laid bare to you,
    My love that you can make not void nor vain,
Love that foregoes you but to claim anew
Beyond this passage of the gate of death,
    I charge you at the Judgment make it plain
My love of you was life and not a breath.

12

'Amor che ne la mente mi ragiona.'—DANTE
'Amor vien nel bel viso di costei.'—PETRARCA

If there be any one can take my place
    And make you happy whom I grieve to grieve,
    Think not that I can grudge it, but believe
I do commend you to that nobler grace,
That readier wit than mine, that sweeter face;
    Yea, since your riches make me rich, conceive
    I too am crowned, while bridal crowns I weave,
And thread the bridal dance with jocund pace.
For if I did not love you, it might be
    That I should grudge you some one dear delight;
        But since the heart is yours that was mine own,
    Your pleasure is my pleasure, right my right,

Your honourable freedom makes me free,
    And you companioned I am not alone.

13

       '*E drizzeremo gli occhi al Primo Amore.*'—DANTE
      '*Ma trovo peso non da le mie braccia.*'—PETRARCA

If I could trust mine own self with your fate,
    Shall I not rather trust it in God's hand?
    Without Whose Will one lily doth not stand,
Nor sparrow fall at his appointed date;
    Who numbereth the innumerable sand,
Who weighs the wind and water with a weight,
To Whom the world is neither small nor great,
    Whose knowledge foreknew every plan we planned.
Searching my heart for all that touches you,
    I find there only love and love's goodwill
Helpless to help and impotent to do,
Of understanding dull, of sight most dim;
And therefore I commend you back to Him
    Whose love your love's capacity can fill.

14

       '*E la Sua Volontade è nostra pace.*'—DANTE
     '*Sol con questi pensier, con altre chiome.*'—PETRARCA

Youth gone, and beauty gone if ever there
    Dwelt beauty in so poor a face as this;
    Youth gone and beauty, what remains of bliss?
I will not bind fresh roses in my hair,
To shame a cheek at best but little fair,—
    Leave youth his roses, who can bear a thorn,—
I will not seek for blossoms anywhere,
    Except such common flowers as blow with corn.

Youth gone and beauty gone, what doth remain?
  The longing of a heart pent up forlorn,
      A silent heart whose silence loves and longs;
      The silence of a heart which sang its songs
  While youth and beauty made a summer morn,
Silence of love that cannot sing again.

DEVOTIONAL
POEMS

An Easter Carol

Spring bursts to-day,
For Christ is risen and all the earth's at play.

Flash forth, thou Sun,
The rain is over and gone, its work is done.

Winter is past,
Sweet Spring is come at last, is come at last.

Bud, Fig and Vine,
Bud, Olive, fat with fruit and oil and wine.

Break forth this morn
In roses, thou but yesterday a thorn.

Uplift thy head,
O pure white Lily through the Winter dead.

Beside your dams
Leap and rejoice, you merry-making Lambs.

All Herds and Flocks
Rejoice, all Beasts of thickets and of rocks.

Sing, Creatures, sing,
Angels and Men and Birds and everything.

All notes of Doves
Fill all our world: this is the time of loves.

From "Some Feasts and Fasts"

EASTER TUESDAY

'Together with my dead body shall they arise.'
    Shall my dead body arise? then amen and yea
On track of a home beyond the uttermost skies
    Together with my dead body shall they.

We know the way: thank God Who hath showed us the way!
    Jesus Christ our Way to beautiful Paradise,
Jesus Christ the Same for ever, the Same to-day.

Five Virgins replenish with oil their lamps, being wise,
    Five Virgins awaiting the Bridegroom watch and pray:
And if I one day spring from my grave to the prize,
    Together with my dead body shall they.

Consider the Lilies of the Field

Flowers preach to us if we will hear: —
The rose saith in the dewy morn:
'I am most fair;
Yet all my loveliness is born
Upon a thorn.'
The poppy saith amid the corn:
'Let but my scarlet head appear
And I am held in scorn;
Yet juice of subtle virtue lies
Within my cup of curious dyes.'
The lilies say: 'Behold how we
Preach without words of purity.'
The violets whisper from the shade
Which their own leaves have made:
'Men scent our fragrance on the air,
Yet take no heed
Of humble lessons we would read.'

But not alone the fairest flowers:
The merest grass
Along the roadside where we pass,
Lichen and moss and sturdy weed,
Tell of His love who sends the dew,
The rain and sunshine too,
To nourish one small seed.

From "*Christ Our All in All*"

The ransomed of the Lord.

Thy lovely saints do bring Thee love,
    Incense and joy and gold;
Fair star with star, fair dove with dove,
    Beloved by Thee of old.
I, Master, neither star nor dove,
    Have brought Thee sins and tears;
Yet I too bring a little love
    Amid my flaws and fears.
A trembling love that faints and fails
    Yet still is love of Thee,
A wondering love that hopes and hails
    Thy boundless Love of me;
Love kindling faith and pure desire,
    Love following on to bliss,
A spark, O Jesus, from Thy fire,
    A drop from Thine abyss.

Holy Innocents

Sleep, little Baby, sleep;
    The holy Angels love thee,
And guard thy bed, and keep
    A blessed watch above thee.
No spirit can come near
    Nor evil beast to harm thee:
Sleep, Sweet, devoid of fear
    Where nothing need alarm thee.

The Love which doth not sleep,
    The eternal Arms surround thee:
The Shepherd of the sheep
    In perfect love hath found thee.
Sleep through the holy night,
    Christ-kept from snare and sorrow,
Until thou wake to light
    And love and warmth to-morrow.

St. Elizabeth of Hungary

When if ever life is sweet,
    Save in heart in all a child,
    A fair virgin undefiled,
Knelt she at her Saviour's feet:
While she laid her royal crown,
    Thinking it too mean a thing
    For a solemn offering,
Careless on the cushions down.

Fair she was as any rose,
    But more pale than lilies white:
Her eyes full of deep repose
    Seemed to see beyond our sight.
Hush, she is a holy thing:
    Hush, her soul is in her eyes,
    Seeking far in Paradise
For her Light, her Love, her King.

The Three Enemies

'Sweet, thou art pale.'
'More pale to see,
Christ hung upon the cruel tree
And bore His Father's wrath for me.'

'Sweet, thou art sad.'
'Beneath a rod
More heavy, Christ for my sake trod
The winepress of the wrath of God.'

'Sweet, thou art weary.'
'Not so Christ;
Whose mighty love of me sufficed
For Strength, Salvation, Eucharist.'

'Sweet, thou art footsore.'
'If I bleed,
His feet have bled; yea in my need
His Heart once bled for mine indeed.'

THE WORLD
'Sweet, thou art young.'
'So He was young
Who for my sake in silence hung
Upon the Cross with Passion wrung.'

'Look, thou art fair.'
　　　　'He was more fair
Than men, Who deigned for me to wear
A visage marred beyond compare.'

'And thou hast riches.'
　　　　'Daily bread:
All else is His: Who, living, dead,
For me lacked where to lay His Head.'

'And life is sweet.'
　　　　'It was not so
To Him, Whose Cup did overflow
With mine unutterable woe.'

THE DEVIL
　　'Thou drinkest deep.'
　　　　'When Christ would sup
He drained the dregs from out my cup:
So how should I be lifted up?'

'Thou shalt win Glory.'
　　　　'In the skies,
Lord Jesus, cover up mine eyes
Lest they should look on vanities.'

'Thou shalt have Knowledge.'
　　　　'Helpless dust!
In thee, O Lord, I put my trust:
Answer Thou for me, Wise and Just.'

'And Might.'—
　　　　'Get thee behind me. Lord,
Who has redeemed and not abhorred
My soul, oh keep it by Thy Word.'

64

From "*Songs for Strangers and Pilgrims*"

Consider the Lilies of the field.

Solomon most glorious in array
    Put not on his glories without care:—
Clothe us as Thy lilies of a day,
    As the lilies Thou accountest fair,
        Lilies of Thy making,
        Of Thy love partaking,
    Filling with free fragrance earth and air:
Thou Who gatherest lilies, gather us and wear.

From "*Songs for Strangers and Pilgrims*"

Lord, grant us calm, if calm can set forth Thee;
    Or tempest, if a tempest set Thee forth;
    Wind from the east or west or south or north,
Or congelation of a silent sea,
With stillness of each tremulous aspen tree.

Still let fruit fall, or hang upon the tree;
    Still let the east and west, the south and north,
Curb in their winds, or plough a thundering sea;
    Still let the earth abide to set Thee forth,
Or vanish like a smoke to set forth Thee.

From "*Songs for Strangers and Pilgrims*"
SURSUM CORDA

'Lift up your hearts.' 'We lift them up.' Ah me!
I cannot, Lord, lift up my heart to Thee:
Stoop, lift it up, that where Thou art I too may be.

'Give Me thy heart.' I would not say Thee nay,
But have no power to keep or give away
My heart: stoop, Lord, and take it to Thyself to-day.

Stoop, Lord, as once before, now once anew;
Stoop, Lord, and hearken, hearken, Lord, and do,
And take my will, and take my heart, and take me too.

Amor Mundi

'Oh where are you going with your love-locks flowing,
    On the west wind blowing along this valley track?'
'The downhill path is easy, come with me an it please ye,
    We shall escape the uphill by never turning back.'

So they two went together in glowing August weather,
    The honey-breathing heather lay to their left and right;
And dear she was to doat on, her swift feet seemed to float on
    The air like soft twin pigeons too sportive to alight.

'Oh what is that in heaven where grey cloud-flakes are seven,
    Where blackest clouds hang riven just at the rainy skirt?'
'Oh, that's a meteor sent us, a message dumb, portentous,
    An undeciphered solemn signal of help or hurt.'

'Oh what is that glides quickly where velvet flowers grow thickly,
    Their scent comes rich and sickly?' 'A scaled and hooded
        worm.'
'Oh what's that in the hollow, so pale I quake to follow?'
    'Oh that's a thin dead body which waits the eternal term.'

'Turn again, O my sweetest,—turn again, false and fleetest:
    This beaten way thou beatest, I fear, is hell's own track.'
'Nay, too steep for hill mounting; nay, too late for cost counting:
    This downhill path is easy, but there's no turning back.'

From *"New Jerusalem and its Citizens"*

*As cold waters to a thirsty soul, so is good
news from a far country.*

'Golden-haired, lily-white,
    Will you pluck me lilies?
Or will you show me where they grow,
    Show where the limpid rill is?
But is your hair of gold or light,
    And is your foot of flake or fire,
And have you wings rolled up from sight
    And songs to slake desire?'

'I pluck fresh flowers of Paradise,
    Lilies and roses red,
A bending sceptre for my hand,
    A crown to crown my head.
I sing my songs, I pluck my flowers
Sweet-scented from their fragrant trees;
I sing, we sing, amid the bowers,
    And gather palm-branches.'

'Is there a path to Heaven
    My stumbling foot may tread?
And will you show that way to go,
    That bower and blossom bed?'
'The path to Heaven is steep and straight
    And scorched, but ends in shade of trees,
Where yet a while we sing and wait
    And gather palm-branches.'

69

From "*Songs for Strangers and Pilgrims*"

Marvel of marvels, if I myself shall behold
With mine own eyes my King in His city of gold;
Where the least of lambs is spotless white in the fold,
Where the least and last of saints in spotless white is stoled,
Where the dimmest head beyond a moon is aureoled.
O saints, my beloved, now mouldering to mould in the mould,
Shall I see you lift your heads, see your cerements unrolled,
See with these very eyes? who now in darkness and cold
Tremble for the midnight cry, the rapture, the tale untold,
'The Bridegroom cometh, cometh, His Bride to enfold.'

Cold it is, my beloved, since your funeral bell was tolled:
Cold it is, O my King, how cold alone on the wold.

Up-Hill

Does the road wind up-hill all the way?
   Yes, to the very end.
Will the day's journey take the whole long day?
   From morn to night, my friend.

But is there for the night a resting-place?
   A roof for when the slow dark hours begin.
May not the darkness hide it from my face?
   You cannot miss that inn.

Shall I meet other wayfarers at night?
   Those who have gone before.
Then must I knock, or call when just in sight?
   They will not keep you standing at that door.

Shall I find comfort, travel-sore and weak?
   Of labour you shall find the sum.
Will there be beds for me and all who seek?
   Yea, beds for all who come.

Good Friday

Am I a stone, and not a sheep,
    That I can stand, O Christ, beneath Thy cross,
    To number drop by drop Thy Blood's slow loss,
And yet not weep?

Not so those women loved
    Who with exceeding grief lamented Thee;
    Not so fallen Peter weeping bitterly;
Not so the thief was moved;

Not so the Sun and Moon
    Which hid their faces in a starless sky,
A horror of great darkness at broad noon—
    I, only I.

Yet give not o'er,
    But seek Thy sheep, true Shepherd of the flock;
Greater than Moses, turn and look once more
    And smite a rock.

A Rose Plant in Jericho

At morn I plucked a rose and gave it to Thee,
    A rose of joy and happy love and peace,
        A rose with scarce a thorn:
        But in the chillness of a second morn
    My rose bush drooped, and all its gay increase
Was but one thorn that wounded me.

I plucked the thorn and offered it to Thee,
    And for my thorn Thou gavest love and peace,
        Not joy this mortal morn:
        If Thou hast given much treasure for a thorn,
    Wilt Thou not give me for my rose increase
Of gladness, and all sweets to me?

My thorny rose, my love and pain, to Thee
    I offer; and I set my heart in peace,
        And rest upon my thorn:
        For verily I think to-morrow morn
    Shall bring me Paradise, my gift's increase,
Yea, give Thy very Self to me.

Despised and Rejected

My sun has set, I dwell
In darkness as a dead man out of sight;
And none remains, not one, that I should tell
To him mine evil plight
This bitter night.
I will make fast my door
That hollow friends may trouble me no more.

'Friend, open to Me.'—'Who is this that calls?
Nay, I am deaf as are my walls:
Cease crying, for I will not hear
Thy cry of hope or fear.
Others were dear,
Others forsook me: what art thou indeed
That I should heed
Thy lamentable need?
Hungry should feed,
Or stranger lodge thee here?'

'Friend, My Feet bleed.
Open thy door to Me and comfort Me.'
'I will not open, trouble me no more.
Go on thy way footsore,
I will not rise and open unto thee.'

'Then is it nothing to thee? Open, see
Who stands to plead with thee.

Open, lest I should pass thee by, and thou
One day entreat my Face
And howl for grace,
And I be deaf as thou art now.
Open to Me.'

Then I cried out upon him: 'Cease,
Leave me in peace:
Fear not that I should crave
Aught thou mayst have.
Leave me in peace, yea trouble me no more.
Lest I arise and chase thee from my door
What, shall I not be let
Alone, that thou dost vex me yet?'

But all night long that voice spake urgently,
'Open to Me.'
Still harping in mine ears:
'Rise, let Me in.'
Pleading with tears:
'Open to Me, that I may come to thee.'
While the dew dropped, while the dark hours were cold:
'My Feet bleed, see My Face,
See My Hands bleed that bring thee grace,
My Heart doth bleed for thee,—
Open to Me.'

So till the break of day:
Then died away
That voice, in silence as of sorrow;
Then footsteps echoing like a sigh
Passed me by,
Lingering footsteps slow to pass.

On the morrow
I saw upon the grass
Each footprint marked in blood, and on my door
The mark of blood for evermore.

Sonnets from *"Later Life"*

11

Lifelong our stumbles, lifelong our regret,
    Lifelong our efforts failing and renewed,
    While lifelong is our witness, 'God is good,'
Who bore with us till now, bears with us yet,
Who still remembers and will not forget,
    Who gives us light and warmth and daily food;
    And gracious promises half understood,
And glories half unveiled, whereon to set
Our heart of hearts and eyes of our desire;
    Uplifting us to longing and to love,
Luring us upward from this world of mire,
    Urging us to press on and mount above
    Ourselves and all we have had experience of,
Mounting to Him in love's perpetual fire.

23

Beyond the seas we know stretch seas unknown,
    Blue and bright-coloured for our dim and green;
    Beyond the lands we see stretch lands unseen
With many-tinted tangle overgrown;
And icebound seas there are like seas of stone,
    Serenely stormless as death lies serene;
    And lifeless tracts of sand, which intervene
Betwixt the lands where living flowers are blown.
This dead and living world befits our case
    Who live and die: we live in wearied hope,

We die in hope not dead; we run a race
To-day, and find no present halting-place;
    All things we see lie far within our scope,
And still we peer beyond with craving face.

From "*They Desire a Better Country*"

11

What seekest thou, far in the unknown land?
   In hope I follow joy gone on before;
   In hope and fear persistent more and more,
As the dry desert lengthens out its sand.
Whilst day and night I carry in my hand
   The golden key to ope the golden door
   Of golden home; yet mine eye weepeth sore,
For long the journey is that makes no stand.
And who is this that veiled doth walk with thee?
   Lo this is Love that walketh at my right;
   One exile holds us both, and we are bound
To selfsame home-joys in the land of light.
Weeping thou walkest with him; weepeth he?
Some sobbing weep, some weep and make no sound.

From "*The World. Self-destruction*"

Lord, save us, we perish.

O Lord, seek us, O Lord, find us
    In Thy patient care;
Be Thy Love before, behind us,
    Round us, everywhere:
Lest the god of this world blind us,
    Lest he speak us fair,
Lest he forge a chain to bind us,
    Lest he bait a snare.
Turn not from us, call to mind us,
    Find, embrace us, bear;
Be Thy Love before, behind us,
    Round us, everywhere.

From "*Gifts and Graces*"

If thou be dead, forgive and thou shalt live;
    If thou hast sinned, forgive and be forgiven;
God waiteth to be gracious and forgive,
    And open heaven.

Set not thy will to die and not to live;
    Set not thy face as flint refusing heaven;
Thou fool, set not thy heart on hell: forgive
    And be forgiven.

From "*Divers Worlds. Time and Eternity*"

Heaven's chimes are slow, but sure to strike at last:
   Earth's sands are slow, but surely dropping thro':
   And much we have to suffer, much to do,
     Before the time be past.

Chimes that keep time are neither slow nor fast:
   Not many are the numbered sands nor few:
   A time to suffer, and a time to do,
     And then the time is past.

Heaven Overarches

Heaven overarches earth and sea,
   Earth-sadness and sea-bitterness.
Heaven overarches you and me:
A little while and we shall be—
Please God—where there is no more sea
   Nor barren wilderness.

Heaven overarches you and me,
   And all earth's gardens and her graves.
Look up with me, until we see
The day break and the shadows flee
What though to-night wrecks you and me
   If so to-morrow saves?

Love Is Strong as Death

'I have not sought Thee, I have not found Thee,
   I have not thirsted for Thee:
And now cold billows of death surround me,
Buffeting billows of death astound me,—
   Wilt Thou look upon, wilt Thou see
   Thy perishing me?'

'Yea, I have sought thee, yea, I have found thee,
   Yea, I have thirsted for thee,
Yea, long ago with love's bands I bound thee:
Now the Everlasting Arms surround thee,—
   Through death's darkness I look and see
   And clasp thee to Me.'

From "*Songs for Strangers and Pilgrims*"

Are they not all Ministering Spirits?

Lord, whomsoever Thou shalt send to me,
    Let that same be
    Mine Angel predilect:
Veiled or unveiled, benignant or austere,
Aloof or near;
    Thine, therefore mine, elect.

So may my soul nurse patience day by day,
Watch on and pray
    Obedient and at peace;
Living a lonely life in hope, in faith;
Loving till death,
    When life, not love, shall cease.

. . . Lo, thou mine Angel with transfigured face
Brimful of grace,
    Brimful of love for me!
Did I misdoubt thee all that weary while,
Thee with a smile
    For me as I for thee?

From *"Christ Our All in All"*

Lord, I am here. —But, child, I look for thee
    Elsewhere and nearer Me.—
Lord, that way moans a wide insatiate sea:
    How can I come to Thee?—
Set foot upon the water, test and see
    If thou canst come to Me.—
Couldst Thou not send a boat to carry me,
    Or dolphin swimming free?—

Nay, boat nor fish if thy will faileth thee:
    For My Will too is free.—
O Lord, I am afraid. —Take hold on Me:
    I am stronger than the sea.—
Save, Lord, I perish. —I have hold of thee.
    I made and rule the sea,
I bring thee to the haven where thou wouldst be.

Sleep at Sea

Sound the deep waters:—
 Who shall sound that deep?—
Too short the plummet,
 And the watchmen sleep.
Some dream of effort
 Up a toilsome steep;
Some dream of pasture grounds
 For harmless sheep.

White shapes flit to and fro
 From mast to mast;
They feel the distant tempest
 That nears them fast:
Great rocks are straight ahead
 Great shoals not past;
They shout to one another
Upon the blast.

Oh soft the streams drop music
 Between the hills,
And musical the birds' nests
 Beside those rills:
The nests are types of home
 Love-hidden from ills,
The nests are types of spirits
 Love-music fills.

So dream the sleepers,
        Each man in his place;
The lightning shows the smile
        Upon each face:
The ship is driving, — driving, —
        It drives apace:
And sleepers smile, and spirits
        Bewail their case.

The lightning glares and reddens
        Across the skies;
It seems but sunset
        To those sleeping eyes.
When did the sun go down
        On such a wise?
From such a sunset
        When shall day arise?

'Wake,' call the spirits:
        But to heedless ears:
They have forgotten sorrows
        And hopes and fears;
They have forgotten perils
        And smiles and tears;
Their dream has held them long,
        Long years and years.

'Wake,' call the spirits again:
        But it would take
A louder summons
        To bid them awake.
Some dream of pleasure
        For another's sake:
Some dream, forgetful
        Of a lifelong ache.

One by one slowly,
    Ah how sad and slow!
Wailing and praying
    The spirits rise and go:
Clear stainless spirits,
    White, as white as snow;
Pale spirits, wailing
    For an overthrow.

One by one flitting,
    Like a mournful bird
Whose song is tired at last
    For no mate heard.
The loving voice is silent,
    The useless word;
One by one flitting
    Sick with hope deferred.

Driving and driving,
    The ship drives amain:
While swift from mast to mast
    Shapes flit again,
Flit silent as the silence
    Where men lie slain;
Their shadow cast upon the sails
    Is like a stain.

No voice to call the sleepers,
    No hand to raise:
They sleep to death in dreaming
    Of length of days.
Vanity of vanities,
    The Preacher says:
Vanity is the end
    Of all their ways.

Pleading

O Lord, I cannot plead my love of Thee:
    I plead Thy Love of me:—
The shallow conduit hails the unfathomed sea.

POEMS
OF NATURE,
EXPERIENCE,
TIME, AND
ETERNITY

Goblin Market

Morning and evening
Maids heard the goblins cry:
"Come buy our orchard fruits,
Come buy, come buy:
Apples and quinces,
Lemons and oranges,
Plump unpecked cherries,
Melons and raspberries,
Bloom-down-cheeked peaches,
Swart-headed mulberries,
Wild free-born cranberries,
Crab-apples, dewberries,
Pine-apples, blackberries,
Apricots, strawberries;—
All ripe together
In summer weather,—
Morns that pass by,
Fair eves that fly;
Come buy, come buy:
Our grapes fresh from the vine,
Pomegranates full and fine,
Dates and sharp bullaces,
Rare pears and greengages,
Damsons and bilberries,
Taste them and try:
Currants and gooseberries,
Bright-fire-like barberries,

Figs to fill your mouth,
Citrons from the South,
Sweet to tongue and sound to eye;
Come buy, come buy."

Evening by evening
Among the brookside rushes,
Laura bowed her head to hear,
Lizzie veiled her blushes:
Crouching close together
In the cooling weather,
With clasping arms and cautioning lips,
With tingling cheeks and finger tips.
"Lie close," Laura said,
Pricking up her golden head:
"We must not look at goblin men,
We must not buy their fruits:
Who knows upon what soil they fed
Their hungry thirsty roots?"
"Come buy," call the goblins
Hobbling down the glen.
"Oh," cried Lizzie, "Laura, Laura,
You should not peep at goblin men."
Lizzie covered up her eyes,
Covered close lest they should look;
Laura reared her glossy head,
And whispered like the restless brook:
"Look, Lizzie, look, Lizzie,
Down the glen tramp little men.
One hauls a basket,
One bears a plate,
One lugs a golden dish
Of many pounds' weight.
How fair the vine must grow
Whose grapes are so luscious;
How warm the wind must blow

Through those fruit bushes."
"No," said Lizzie: "No, no, no;
Their offers should not charm us,
Their evil gifts would harm us."
She thrust a dimpled finger
In each ear, shut eyes and ran:
Curious Laura chose to linger
Wondering at each merchant man.
One had a cat's face,
One whisked a tail,
One tramped at a rat's pace,
One crawled like a snail,
One like a wombat prowled obtuse and furry,
One like a ratel tumbled hurry skurry.
She heard a voice like voice of doves
Cooing all together:
They sounded kind and full of loves
In the pleasant weather.

     Laura stretched her gleaming neck
Like a rush-imbedded swan,
Like a lily from the beck,
Like a moonlit poplar branch,
Like a vessel at the launch
When its last restraint is gone.

     Backwards up the mossy glen
Turned and trooped the goblin men,
With their shrill repeated cry,
"Come buy, come buy."
When they reached where Laura was
They stood stock still upon the moss,
Leering at each other,
Brother with queer brother;
Signalling each other,
Brother with sly brother.
One set his basket down,

One reared his plate;
One began to weave a crown
Of tendrils, leaves, and rough nuts brown
(Men sell not such in any town);
One heaved the golden weight
Of dish and fruit to offer her:
"Come buy, come buy," was still their cry.
Laura stared but did not stir,
Longed but had no money:
The whisk-tailed merchant bade her taste
In tones as smooth as honey,
The cat-faced purr'd,
The rat-paced spoke a word
Of welcome, and the snail-paced even was heard;
One parrot-voiced and jolly
Cried "Pretty Goblin" still for "Pretty Polly";—
One whistled like a bird.

But sweet-tooth Laura spoke in haste:
"Good folk, I have no coin;
To take were to purloin:
I have no copper in my purse,
I have no silver either,
And all my gold is on the furze
That shakes in windy weather
Above the rusty heather."
"You have much gold upon your head,"
They answered all together:
"Buy from us with a golden curl."
She clipped a precious golden lock,
She dropped a tear more rare than pearl,
Then sucked their fruit globes fair or red:
Sweeter than honey from the rock,
Stronger than man-rejoicing wine,
Clearer than water flowed that juice;
She never tasted such before,

How should it cloy with length of use?
She sucked and sucked and sucked the more
Fruits which that unknown orchard bore;
She sucked until her lips were sore;
Then flung the emptied rinds away
But gathered up one kernel-stone,
And knew not was it night or day
As she turned home alone.

Lizzie met her at the gate
Full of wise upbraidings:
"Dear, you should not stay so late,
Twilight is not good for maidens;
Should not loiter in the glen
In the haunts of goblin men.
Do you not remember Jeanie,
How she met them in the moonlight,
Took their gifts both choice and many,
Ate their fruits and wore their flowers
Plucked from bowers
Where summer ripens at all hours?
But ever in the noonlight
She pined and pined away;
Sought them by night and day,
Found them no more, but dwindled and grew grey;
Then fell with the first snow,
While to this day no grass will grow
Where she lies low:
I planted daisies there a year ago
That never blow.
You should not loiter so."
"Nay, hush," said Laura:
"Nay, hush, my sister:
I ate and ate my fill,
Yet my mouth waters still;
To-morrow night I will

Buy more": and kissed her:
"Have done with sorrow;
I'll bring you plums to-morrow
Fresh on their mother twigs,
Cherries worth getting;
You cannot think what figs
My teeth have met in,
What melons icy-cold
Piled on a dish of gold
Too huge for me to hold,
What peaches with a velvet nap,
Pellucid grapes without one seed:
Odorous indeed must be the mead
Whereon they grow, and pure the wave they drink
With lilies at the brink,
And sugar-sweet their sap."

Golden head by golden head,
Like two pigeons in one nest,
Folded in each other's wings,
They lay down in their curtained bed:
Like two blossoms on one stem,
Like two flakes of new-fall'n snow,
Like two wands of ivory
Tipped with gold for awful kings.
Moon and stars gazed in at them,
Wind sang to them lullaby,
Lumbering owls forbore to fly,
Not a bat flapped to and fro
Round their nest:
Cheek to cheek and breast to breast
Locked together in one nest.

Early in the morning
When the first cock crowed his warning,
Neat like bees, as sweet and busy,

Laura rose with Lizzie:
Fetched in honey, milked the cows,
Aired and set to rights the house,
Kneaded cakes of whitest wheat,
Cakes for dainty mouths to eat,
Next churned butter, whipped up cream,
Fed their poultry, sat and sewed;
Talked as modest maidens should:
Lizzie with an open heart,
Laura in an absent dream,
One content, one sick in part;
One warbling for the mere bright day's delight,
One longing for the night.

At length slow evening came:
They went with pitchers to the reedy brook;
Lizzie most placid in her look,
Laura most like a leaping flame.
They drew the gurgling water from its deep;
Lizzie plucked purple and rich golden flags,
Then turning homewards said: "The sunset flushes
Those furthest loftiest crags;
Come, Laura, not another maiden lags,
No wilful squirrel wags,
The beasts and birds are fast asleep."
But Laura loitered still among the rushes
And said the bank was steep.

And said the hour was early still,
The dew not fall'n, the wind not chill:
Listening ever, but not catching
The customary cry,
"Come buy, come buy,"
With its iterated jingle
Of sugar-baited words:
Not for all her watching

Once discerning even one goblin
Racing, whisking, tumbling, hobbling;
Let alone the herds
That used to tramp along the glen,
In groups or single,
Of brisk fruit-merchant men.

Till Lizzie urged, "O Laura, come;
I hear the fruit-call, but I dare not look:
You should not loiter longer at this brook:
Come with me home.
The stars rise, the moon bends her arc,
Each glowworm winks her spark,
Let us get home before the night grows dark:
For clouds may gather
Though this is summer weather,
Put out the lights and drench us through;
Then if we lost our way what should we do?"

Laura turned cold as stone
To find her sister heard that cry alone,
That goblin cry,
"Come buy our fruits, come buy."
Must she then buy no more such dainty fruit?
Must she no more such succous pasture find,
Gone deaf and blind?
Her tree of life drooped from the root:
She said not one word in her heart's sore ache;
But peering thro' the dimness, naught discerning,
Trudged home, her pitcher dripping all the way;
So crept to bed, and lay
Silent till Lizzie slept;
Then sat up in a passionate yearning,
And gnashed her teeth for baulked desire, and wept
As if her heart would break.

Day after day, night after night,
Laura kept watch in vain
In sullen silence of exceeding pain.
She never caught again the goblin cry:
"Come buy, come buy";—
She never spied the goblin men
Hawking their fruits along the glen:
But when the moon waxed bright
Her hair grew thin and grey;
She dwindled, as the fair full moon doth turn
To swift decay and burn
Her fire away.

One day remembering her kernel-stone
She set it by a wall that faced the south;
Dewed it with tears, hoped for a root,
Watched for a waxing shoot,
But there came none;
It never saw the sun,
It never felt the trickling moisture run:
While with sunk eyes and faded mouth
She dreamed of melons, as a traveller sees
False waves in desert drouth
With shade of leaf-crowned trees,
And burns the thirstier in the sandful breeze.

She no more swept the house,
Tended the fowls or cows,
Fetched honey, kneaded cakes of wheat,
Brought water from the brook:
But sat down listless in the chimney-nook
And would not eat.

Tender Lizzie could not bear
To watch her sister's cankerous care

Yet not to share.
She night and morning
Caught the goblins' cry:
"Come buy our orchard fruits,
Come buy, come buy": —
Beside the brook, along the glen,
She heard the tramp of goblin men,
The voice and stir
Poor Laura could not hear;
Longed to buy fruit to comfort her,
But feared to pay too dear.
She thought of Jeanie in her grave,
Who should have been a bride;
But who for joys brides hope to have
Fell sick and died
In her gay prime,
In earliest Winter time,
With the first glazing rime,
With the first snow-fall of crisp Winter time.

Till Laura dwindling
Seemed knocking at Death's door:
Then Lizzie weighed no more
Better and worse;
But put a silver penny in her purse,
Kissed Laura, crossed the heath with clumps of furze
At twilight, halted by the brook:
And for the first time in her life
Began to listen and look.

Laughed every goblin
When they spied her peeping:
Came towards her hobbling,
Flying, running, leaping,
Puffing and blowing,
Chuckling, clapping, crowing,

Clucking and gobbling,
Mopping and mowing,
Full of airs and graces,
Pulling wry faces,
Demure grimaces,
Cat-like and rat-like,
Ratel- and wombat-like,
Snail-paced in a hurry,
Parrot-voiced and whistler,
Helter skelter, hurry skurry,
Chattering like magpies,
Fluttering like pigeons,
Gliding like fishes,—
Hugged her and kissed her,
Squeezed and caressed her:
Stretched up their dishes,
Panniers, and plates:
"Look at our apples
Russet and dun,
Bob at our cherries,
Bite at our peaches,
Citrons and dates,
Grapes for the asking,
Pears red with basking
Out in the sun,
Plums on their twigs;
Pluck them and suck them,
Pomegranates, figs."—

"Good folk," said Lizzie,
Mindful of Jeanie:
"Give me much and many":—
Held out her apron,
Tossed them her penny.
"Nay, take a seat with us,
Honour and eat with us,"

They answered grinning:
"Our feast is but beginning.
Night yet is early,
Warm and dew-pearly,
Wakeful and starry:
Such fruits as these
No man can carry;
Half their bloom would fly,
Half their dew would dry,
Half their flavour would pass by.
Sit down and feast with us,
Be welcome guest with us,
Cheer you and rest with us."—
"Thank you," said Lizzie: "But one waits
At home alone for me:
So without further parleying,
If you will not sell me any
Of your fruits though much and many,
Give me back my silver penny
I tossed you for a fee."—
They began to scratch their pates,
No longer wagging, purring,
But visibly demurring,
Grunting and snarling.
One called her proud,
Cross-grained, uncivil;
Their tones waxed loud,
Their looks were evil.
Lashing their tails
They trod and hustled her,
Elbowed and jostled her,
Clawed with their nails,
Barking, mewing, hissing, mocking,
Tore her gown and soiled her stocking,
Twitched her hair out by the roots,
Stamped upon her tender feet,

Held her hands and squeezed their fruits
Against her mouth to make her eat.

White and golden Lizzie stood,
Like a lily in a flood,—
Like a rock of blue-veined stone
Lashed by tides obstreperously,—
Like a beacon left alone
In a hoary roaring sea,
Sending up a golden fire,—
Like a fruit-crowned orange-tree,
White with blossoms honey-sweet,
Sore beset by wasp and bee,—
Like a royal virgin town
Topped with gilded dome and spire
Close beleaguered by a fleet
Mad to tug her standard down.

One may lead a horse to water,
Twenty cannot make him drink.
Though the goblins cuffed and caught her,
Coaxed and fought her,
Bullied and besought her,
Scratched her, pinched her black as ink,
Kicked and knocked her,
Mauled and mocked her,
Lizzie uttered not a word;
Would not open lip from lip
Lest they should cram a mouthful in:
But laughed in heart to feel the drip
Of juice that syruped all her face,
And lodged in dimples of her chin,
And streaked her neck which quaked like curd.
At last the evil people
Worn out by her resistance
Flung back her penny, kicked their fruit

Along whichever road they took,
Not leaving root or stone or shoot;
Some writhed into the ground,
Some dived into the brook
With ring and ripple,
Some scudded on the gale without a sound,
Some vanished in the distance.

In a smart, ache, tingle,
Lizzie went her way;
Knew not was it night or day;
Sprang up the bank, tore thro' the furze,
Threaded copse and dingle;
And heard her penny jingle
Bouncing in her purse,—
Its bounce was music to her ear.
She ran and run
As if she feared some goblin man
Dogged her with gibe or curse
Or something worse:
But not one goblin skurried after,
Nor was she pricked by fear;
The kind heart made her windy-paced
That urged her home quite out of breath with haste
And inward laughter.

She cried, "Laura," up the garden,
"Did you miss me?
Come and kiss me.
Never mind my bruises,
Hug me, kiss me, suck my juices
Squeezed from goblin fruits for you,
Goblin pulp and goblin dew.
Eat me, drink me, love me;
Laura, make much of me:

For your sake I have braved the glen
And had to do with goblin merchant men."

Laura started from her chair,
Flung her arms up in the air,
Clutched her hair:
"Lizzie, Lizzie, have you tasted
For my sake the fruit forbidden?
Must your light like mine be hidden,
Your young life like mine be wasted,
Undone in mine undoing
And ruined in my ruin,
Thirsty, cankered, goblin-ridden?"—
She clung about her sister,
Kissed and kissed and kissed her:
Tears once again
Refreshed her shrunken eyes,
Dropping like rain
After long sultry drouth;
Shaking with anguish, fear, and pain,
She kissed and kissed her with a hungry mouth.

Her lips began to scorch,
That juice was wormwood to her tongue,
She loathed the feast:
Writhing as one possessed she leaped and sung,
Rent all her robe, and wrung
Her hands in lamentable haste,
And beat her breast.
Her locks streamed like the torch
Borne by a racer at full speed,
Or like the mane of horses in their flight,
Or like an eagle when she stems the light
Straight toward the sun,
Or like a caged thing freed,
Or like a flying flag when armies run.

Swift fire spread through her veins, knocked at her heart,
Met the fire smouldering there
And overbore its lesser flame;
She gorged on bitterness without a name:
Ah! fool, to choose such part
Of soul-consuming care!
Sense failed in the mortal strife:
Like the watch-tower of a town
Which an earthquake shatters down,
Like a lightning-stricken mast,
Like a wind-uprooted tree
Spun about,
Like a foam-topped waterspout
Cast down headlong in the sea,
She fell at last;
Pleasure past and anguish past,
Is it death or is it life?

Life out of death.
That night long Lizzie watched by her,
Counted her pulse's flagging stir,
Felt for her breath,
Held water to her lips, and cooled her face
With tears and fanning leaves:
But when the first birds chirped about their eaves,
And early reapers plodded to the place
Of golden sheaves,
And dew-wet grass
Bowed in the morning winds so brisk to pass,
And new buds with new day
Opened of cup-like lilies on the stream,
Laura awoke as from a dream,
Laughed in the innocent old way,
Hugged Lizzie but not twice or thrice;
Her gleaming locks showed not one thread of grey,

Her breath was sweet as May
And light danced in her eyes.

Days, weeks, months, years,
Afterwards, when both were wives
With children of their own;
Their mother-hearts beset with fears,
Their lives bound up in tender lives;
Laura would call the little ones
And tell them of her early prime,
Those pleasant days long gone
Of not-returning time:
Would talk about the haunted glen,
The wicked quaint fruit-merchant men,
Their fruits like honey to the throat
But poison in the blood;
(Men sell not such in any town:)
Would tell them how her sister stood
In deadly peril to do her good,
And win the fiery antidote:
Then joining hands to little hands
Would bid them cling together,
"For there is no friend like a sister
In calm or stormy weather;
To cheer one on the tedious way,
To fetch one if one goes astray,
To lift one if one totters down,
To strengthen whilst one stands."

Queen Rose

The jessamine shows like a star;
  The lilies sway like sceptres slim;
Fair clematis from near and far
  Sets forth its wayward tangled whim;

  Curved meadowsweet blooms rich and dim;—
But yet a rose is fairer far.

The jessamine is odorous; so
  Maid-lilies are, and clematis;
And where tall meadowsweet flowers grow
  A rare and subtle perfume is;—
  What can there be more choice than these?—
A rose when it doth bud and blow.

Let others choose sweet jessamine,
  Or weave their lily-crown aright,
And let who love it pluck and twine
  Loose clematis, or draw delight
  From meadowsweets' cluster downy white—
The rose, the perfect rose, be mine.

Song

Oh roses for the flush of youth,
    And laurel for the perfect prime;
But pluck an ivy branch for me
    Grown old before my time.

Oh violets for the grave of youth,
    And bay for those dead in their prime;
Give me the withered leaves I chose
    Before in the old time.

Immalee

I gather thyme upon the sunny hills,
    And its pure fragrance ever gladdens me,
    And in my mind having tranquillity
I smile to see how my green basket fills.
And by clear streams I gather daffodils;
    And in dim woods find out the cherry-tree,
    And take its fruit and the wild strawberry
And nuts and honey; and live free from ills.
I dwell on the green earth, 'neath the blue sky,
    Birds are my friends, and leaves my rustling roof:
The deer are not afraid of me, and I
    Hear the wild goat, and hail its hastening hoof;
The squirrels sit perked as I pass them by,
    And even the watchful hare stands not aloof.

From "*Songs for Strangers and Pilgrims*"

Where shall I find a white rose blowing?—
 Out in the garden where all sweets be.—
But out in my garden the snow was snowing
 And never a white rose opened for me.
Nought but snow and a wind were blowing
 And snowing.

Where shall I find a blush rose blushing?—
 On the garden wall or the garden bed.—
But out in my garden the rain was rushing
 And never a blush rose raised its head.
Nothing glowing, flushing or blushing:
 Rain rushing.

Where shall I find a red rose budding?—
 Out in the garden where all things grow.—
But out in my garden a flood was flooding
 And never a red rose began to blow.
Out in a flooding what should be budding?
 All flooding!

Now is winter and now is sorrow,
 No roses but only thorns to-day:
Thorns will put on roses to-morrow,
 Winter and sorrow scudding away.
No more winter and no more sorrow
 To-morrow.

Symbols

I watched a rosebud very long
 Brought on by dew and sun and shower,
 Waiting to see the perfect flower:
Then, when I thought it should be strong,
 It opened at the matin hour
And fell at evensong.

I watched a nest from day to day,
 A green nest full of pleasant shade,
 Wherein three speckled eggs were laid:
But when they should have hatched in May,
 The two old birds had grown afraid
Or tired, and flew away.

Then in my wrath I broke the bough
 That I had tended so with care,
 Hoping its scent should fill the air;
I crushed the eggs, not heeding how
 Their ancient promise had been fair:
I would have vengeance now.

But the dead branch spoke from the sod,
And the eggs answered me again:
Because we failed dost thou complain?
Is thy wrath just? And what if God,
Who waiteth for thy fruits in vain,
Should also take the rod?

Spring Quiet

Gone were but the Winter,
    Come were but the Spring,
I would go to a covert
    Where the birds sing;

Where in the whitethorn
    Singeth a thrush,
And a robin sings
    In the holly-bush.

Full of fresh scents
    Are the budding boughs
Arching high over
    A cool green house;

Full of sweet scents,
    And whispering air
Which sayeth softly:
    'We spread no snare;

'Here dwell in safety,
    Here dwell alone,
With a clear stream
    And a mossy stone.

'Here the sun shineth
    Most shadily;

Here is heard an echo
Of the far sea,
Though far off it be.'

Dream Land

Where sunless rivers weep
Their waves into the deep,
She sleeps a charmèd sleep:
    Awake her not.
Led by a single star,
She came from very far
To seek where shadows are
    Her pleasant lot.

She left the rosy morn,
She left the fields of corn,
For twilight cold and lorn
    And water springs.
Through sleep, as through a veil
She sees the sky look pale,
And hears the nightingale
    That sadly sings.

Rest, rest, a perfect rest
Shed over brow and breast;
Her face is toward the west,
    The purple land.
She cannot see the grain
Ripening on hill and plain,
She cannot feel the rain
    Upon her hand.

Rest, rest, for evermore
Upon a mossy shore;
Rest, rest at the heart's core
    Till time shall cease:
Sleep that no pain shall wake;
Night that no morn shall break,
Till joy shall overtake
    Her perfect peace.

Cobwebs

It is a land with neither night nor day,
    Nor heat nor cold, nor any wind nor rain,
    Nor hills nor valleys: but one even plain
Stretches through long unbroken miles away,
While through the sluggish air a twilight grey
    Broodeth: no moons or seasons wax and wane,
    No ebb and flow are there along the main,
No bud-time, no leaf-falling, there for aye:—
No ripple on the sea, no shifting sand,
    No beat of wings to stir the stagnant space:
No pulse of life through all the loveless land
And loveless sea; no trace of days before,
    No guarded home, no toil-won resting-place,
No future hope, no fear for ever-more.

A Chilly Night

I rose at the dead of night,
    And went to the lattice alone
To look for my Mother's ghost
    Where the ghostly moonlight shone.

My friends had failed one by one,
    Middle-aged, young, and old,
Till the ghosts were warmer to me
    Than my friends that had grown cold.

I looked and I saw the ghosts
    Dotting plain and mound:
They stood in the blank moonlight,
    But no shadow lay on the ground:
They spoke without a voice
    And they leaped without a sound.

I called: 'O my Mother dear,'—
    I sobbed: 'O my Mother kind,
Make a lonely bed for me
    And shelter it from the wind.

'Tell the others not to come
    To see me night or day:
But I need not tell my friends
    To be sure to keep away.'

My Mother raised her eyes,
    They were blank and could not see:
Yet they held me with their stare
    While they seemed to look at me.

She opened her mouth and spoke;
    I could not hear a word,
While my flesh crept on my bones
    And every hair was stirred.

She knew that I could not hear
    The message that she told
Whether I had long to wait
    Or soon should sleep in the mould:
I saw her toss her shadowless hair
    And wring her hands in the cold.

I strained to catch her words,
    And she strained to make me hear;
But never a sound of words
    Fell on my straining ear.

From midnight to the cockcrow
    I kept my watch in pain
While the subtle ghosts grew subtler
    In the sad night on the wane.

From midnight to the cockcrow
    I watched till all were gone,
Some to sleep in the shifting sea
    And some under turf and stone:
Living had failed and dead had failed,
    And I was indeed alone.

At Home

When I was dead, my spirit turned
    To seek the much-frequented house.
I passed the door, and saw my friends
    Feasting beneath green orange-boughs;
From hand to hand they pushed the wine,
    They sucked the pulp of plum and peach;
They sang, they jested, and they laughed,
    For each was loved of each.

I listened to their honest chat.
    Said one; 'Tomorrow we shall be
Plod plod along the featureless sands,
    And coasting miles and miles of sea.'
Said one: 'Before the turn of tide
    We will achieve the eyrie-seat.'
Said one: 'To-morrow shall be like
    To-day, but much more sweet.'

'To-morrow,' said they, strong with hope,
    And dwelt upon the pleasant way:
'To-morrow,' cried they one and all,
    While no one spoke of yesterday.
Their life stood full at blessed noon;
    I, only I, had passed away:
'To-morrow and to-day,' they cried;
    I was of yesterday.

I shivered comfortless, but cast
    No chill across the tablecloth;
I all-forgotten shivered, sad
    To stay and yet to part how loth:
I passed from the familiar room,
    I who from love had passed away,
Like the remembrance of a guest
    That tarrieth but a day.

From *"Three Stages"*

I. A PAUSE OF THOUGHT

I looked for that which is not, nor can be,
  And hope deferred made my heart sick in truth:
  But years must pass before a hope of youth
    Is resigned utterly.

I watched and waited with a steadfast will:
  And though the object seemed to flee away
  That I so longed for, ever day by day
    I watched and waited still.

Sometimes I said: 'This thing shall be no more;
  My expectation wearies and shall cease;
  I will resign it now and be at peace':
    Yet never gave it o'er.

Sometimes I said: 'It is an empty name
  I long for; to a name why should I give
  The peace of all the days I have to live?'—
    Yet gave it all the same.

Alas thou foolish one! alike unfit
  For healthy joy and salutary pain:
  Thou knowest the case useless, and again
    Turnest to follow it.

From "*Divers Worlds. Time and Eternity*"

Time lengthening, in the lengthening seemeth long:
　　But ended Time will seem a little space,
A little while from morn to evensong,
　　A little while that ran a rapid race;
A little while, when once Eternity
　　Denies proportion to the other's pace.
Eternity to be and be and be,
　　Ever beginning, never ending still,
Still undiminished far as thought can see;
　　Farther than thought can see, by dint of will
Strung up and strained and shooting like a star
Past utmost bound of everlasting hill:
Eternity unswaddled, without bar,
　　Finishing sequence in its awful sum;
Eternity still rolling forth its car,
　　Eternity still here and still to come.

The World

By day she woos me, soft, exceeding fair:
    But all night as the moon so changeth she;
    Loathsome and foul with hideous leprosy,
And subtle serpents gliding in her hair.
By day she woos me to the outer air,
    Ripe fruits, sweet flowers, and full satiety:
    But thro' the night a beast she grins at me,
A very monster void of love and prayer,
By day she stands a lie: by night she stands
    In all the naked horror of the truth,
With pushing horns and clawed and clutching hands.
Is this a friend indeed, that I should sell
    My soul to her, give her my life and youth,
Till my feet, cloven too, take hold on hell?

A Soul

She stands as pale as Parian statues stand;
    Like Cleopatra when she turned at bay,
    And felt her strength above the Roman sway,
And felt the aspic writhing in her hand.
Her face is steadfast toward the shadowy land,
    For dim beyond it looms the land of day:
    Her feet are steadfast, all the arduous way
That foot-track doth not waver on the sand.
She stands there like a beacon through the night,
    A pale clear beacon where the storm-drift is—
She stands alone, a wonder deathly-white:
She stands there patient nerved with inner might,
    Indomitable in her feebleness,
Her face and will athirst against the light.

From the Antique

The wind shall lull us yet,
    The flowers shall spring above us:
And those who hate forget,
    And those forget who love us.

The pulse of hope shall cease,
    Of joy and of regretting:
We twain shall sleep in peace,
    Forgotten and forgetting.

For us no sun shall rise,
    Nor wind rejoice, nor river,
Where we with fast-closed eyes
    Shall sleep and sleep for ever.

En Route

Wherefore art thou strange, and not my mother?
Thou hast stolen my heart and broken it:
Would that I might call thy sons 'My brother,'
    Call thy daughters 'Sister sweet':
Lying in thy lap, not in another,
      Dying at thy feet.

    Farewell, land of love, Italy,
    Sister-land of Paradise:
With mine own feet I have trodden thee,
    Have seen with mine own eyes:
I remember, thou forgettest me,
    I remember thee.

Blessed be the land that warms my heart,
    And the kindly clime that cheers,
And the cordial faces clear from art,
    And the tongue sweet in mine ears:
Take my heart, its truest tenderest part,
    Dear land, take my tears.

A Triad

Three sang of love together: one with lips
    Crimson, with cheeks and bosom in a glow,
Flushed to the yellow hair and finger-tips;
    And one there sang who soft and smooth as snow
    Bloomed like a tinted hyacinth at a show;
And one was blue with famine after love,
    Who like a harpstring snapped rang harsh and low
The burden of what those were singing of.
One shamed herself in love; one temperately
    Grew gross in soulless love, a sluggish wife;
One famished died for love. Thus two of three
    Took death for love and won him after strife;
One droned in sweetness like a fattened bee:
    All on the threshold, yet all short of life.

From *"To-Day and To-Morrow"*

2

I wish I were dead, my foe,
My friend I wish I were dead,
With a stone at my tired feet
And a stone at my tired head.

In the pleasant April days
Half the world will stir and sing,
But half the world will slug and rot
For all the sap of Spring.

Amen

It is over. What is over?
    Nay, now much is over truly!—
Harvest days we toiled to sow for;
    Now the sheaves are gathered newly,
    Now the wheat is garnered duly.

It is finished. What is finished?
Much is finished known or unknown:
Lives are finished; time diminished;
    Was the fallow field left unsown?
    Will these buds be always unblown?

It suffices. What suffices?
    All suffices reckoned rightly:
Spring shall bloom where now the ice is,
    Roses make the bramble sightly,
    And the quickening sun shine brightly,
    And the latter wind blow lightly,
And my garden teem with spices.

From "Some Feasts and Fasts"
MAUNDY THURSDAY

'And the Vine said . . . Should I leave my wine which cheereth
God and man, and go to be promoted over the trees?'

The great Vine left its glory to reign as Forest King.
'Nay,' quoth the lofty forest trees, 'we will not have this thing;
We will not have this supple one enring us with its ring.
Lo from immemorial time our might towers shadowing:
Not we were born to curve and droop, not we to climb and cling:
We buffet back the buffeting wind, tough to its buffeting:
We screen great beasts, the wild fowl build in our heads and
     sing,
Every bird of every feather from our tops takes wing:
I a king, and thou a king, and what king shall be our king?'

Nevertheless the great Vine stooped to be the Forest King,
While the forest swayed and murmured like seas that are
     tempesting:
Stooped and drooped with thousand tendrils in thirsty lan-
     guishing:
Bowed to earth and lay on earth for earth's replenishing;
Put off sweetness, tasted bitterness, endured time's fashioning;
Put off life and put on death:—and lo it was all to bring
All its fellows down to a death which hath lost the sting,
All its fellows up to a life in endless triumphing,—
I a king, and thou a king, and this King to be our King.

133

From "*Songs for Strangers and Pilgrims*"

Heaviness may endure for a night, but
Joy cometh in the morning.

No thing is great on this side of the grave,
    Nor any thing of any stable worth:
    Whatso is born from earth returns to earth:
No thing we grasp proves half the thing we crave:
The tidal wave shrinks to the ebbing wave:
    Laughter is folly, madness lurks in mirth:
    Mankind sets off a-dying from the birth:
Life is a losing game, with what to save?
Thus I sat mourning like a mournful owl,
    And like a doleful dragon made ado,
        Companion of all monsters of the dark:
When lo the light cast off its nightly cowl,
        And up to heaven flashed a carolling lark,
    And all creation sang its hymn anew.

While all creation sang its hymn anew
    What could I do but sing a stave in tune?
    Spectral on high hung pale the vanishing moon
Where a last gleam of stars hung paling too.
Lark's lay—a cockcrow—with a scattered few
    Soft early chirpings—with a tender croon
    Of doves—a hundred thousand calls, and soon
A hundred thousand answers sweet and true.
These set me singing too at unawares:
    One note for all delights and charities,

One note for hope reviving with the light,
One note for every lovely thing that is;
Till while I sang my heart shook off its cares
And revelled in the land of no more night.

A Portrait

1

She gave up beauty in her tender youth,
    Gave all her hope and joy and pleasant ways;
    She covered up her eyes lest they should gaze
On vanity, and chose the bitter truth.
Harsh towards herself, towards others full of ruth,
    Servant of servants, little known to praise,
    Long prayers and fasts trenched on her nights and days:
She schooled herself to sights and sounds uncouth
That with the poor and stricken she might make
    A home, until the least of all sufficed
Her wants; her own self learned she to forsake,
Counting all earthly gain but hurt and loss.
So with calm will she chose and bore the cross
    And hated all for love of Jesus Christ.

2

They knelt in silent anguish by her bed,
    And could not weep; but calmly there she lay.
    All pain had left her; and the sun's last ray
Shone through upon her, warming into red
The shady curtains. In her heart she said:
    'Heaven opens; I leave these and go away;
    The Bridegroom calls,—shall the Bride seek to stay?'
Then low upon her breast she bowed her head.

O lily flower, O gem of priceless worth,
 O dove with patient voice and patient eyes,
O fruitful vine amid a land of dearth,
 O maid replete with loving purities,
Thou bowedst down thy head with friends on earth
 To raise it with the saints in Paradise.

A Life's Parallels

Never on this side of the grave again,
    On this side of the river,
On this side of the garner of the grain,
    Never.

Ever while time flows on and on and on,
    That narrow noiseless river,
Ever while corn bows heavy-headed, wan,
    Ever.

Never despairing, often fainting, rueing,
    But looking back, ah never!
Faint yet pursuing, faint yet still pursuing
    Ever.

CHILDREN'S
VERSES FROM
SING-SONG,
1872

From "*Sing-Song*"

Minnie bakes oaten cakes,
 Minnie brews ale,
All because her Johnny's coming
 Home from sea.
And she glows like a rose,
 Who was so pale,
And 'Are you sure the church clock goes?'
 Says she.

* * *

Rosy maiden Winifred,
With a milkpail on her head,
Tripping through the corn,
 While the dew lies on the wheat
In the sunny morn.
Scarlet shepherd's-weatherglass
 Spreads wide open at her feet
  As they pass;
Cornflowers give their almond smell
 While she brushes by,
 And a lark sings from the sky
  'All is well.'

*　　*　　*

A ring upon her finger,
　　Walks the bride,
With the bridegroom tall and handsome
　　At her side.

A veil upon her forehead,
　　Walks the bride,
With the bridegroom proud and merry
　　At her side.

Fling flowers beneath the footsteps
　　Of the bride;
Fling flowers before the bridegroom
　　At her side.

*　　*　　*

Who has seen the wind?
　　Neither I nor you:
But when the leaves hang trembling
　　The wind is passing thro'.

Who has seen the wind?
　　Neither you nor I:
But when the trees bow down their heads
　　The wind is passing by.

*　　*　　*

An emerald is as green as grass;
      A ruby red as blood;
A sapphire shines as blue as heaven;
      A flint lies in the mud.

A diamond is a brilliant stone,
      To catch the world's desire;
An opal holds a fiery spark;
      But a flint holds fire.

*   *   *

All the bells were ringing
      And all the birds were singing,
When Molly sat down crying
      For her broken doll:
      O you silly Moll!
Sobbing and sighing
      For a broken doll,
When all the bells are ringing
And all the birds are singing.

*   *   *

Wee, wee husband,
      Give me some money.
I have no comfits,
      And I have no honey.

Wee wee wifie,
      I have no money,
Milk, nor meat, nor bread to eat,
      Comfits, nor honey.

*　　*　　*

What does the bee do?
　　Bring home honey.
And what does Father do?
　　Bring home money.
And what does Mother do?
　　Lay out the money.
And what does baby do?
　　Eat up the honey.

*　　*　　*

Dead in the cold, a song-singing thrush,
Dead at the foot of a snowberry bush,—
Weave him a coffin of rush,
Dig him a grave where the soft mosses grow,
Raise him a tombstone of snow.

*　　*　　*

I dug and dug amongst the snow,
And thought the flowers would never grow;
I dug and dug amongst the sand,
And still no green thing came to hand.

Melt, O snow! the warm winds blow
To thaw the flowers and melt the snow;
But all the winds from every land
Will rear no blossom from the sand.

Your brother has a falcon,
　　Your sister has a flower;
But what is left for mannikin,
　　Born within an hour?

I'll nurse you on my knee, my knee,
　　My own little son;
I'll rock you, rock you, in my arms,
　　My least little one.

*   *   *

'Twist me a crown of wind-flowers;
　　That I may fly away
To hear the singers at their song,
　　And players at their play.'

'Put on your crown of wind-flowers:
　　But whither would you go?'
'Beyond the surging of the sea
　　And the storms that blow.'

'Alas! your crown of wind-flowers
　　Can never make you fly:
I twist them in a crown to-day,
　　And to-night they die.'

*   *   *

January cold desolate;
February all dripping wet;
March wind ranges;
April changes;
Birds sing in tune
        To flowers of May,
And sunny June
        Brings longest day;
In scorched July
The storm-clouds fly
Lightning-torn;
August brings corn,
September fruit;
In rough October
Earth must disrobe her;
Stars fall and shoot
In keen November;
And night is long
And cold is strong
In bleak December.

*   *   *

I am a King,
        Or an Emperor rather,
I wear crown-imperial
        And prince's feather;
Golden-rod is the sceptre
        I wield and wag,
And a broad purple flag-flower
        Waves for my flag.

Elder the pithy
        With old-man and sage,

146

These are my councillors
    Green in old age;
Lords-and-ladies in silence
    Stand round me and wait,
While gay ragged-robin
    Makes bows at my gate.

*　　*　　*

Oh fair to see
Bloom-laden cherry tree,
    Arrayed in sunny white
    An April day's delight;
Oh fair to see.

Oh fair to see
Fruit-laden cherry tree,
    With balls of shining red
    Decking a leafy head;
Oh fair to see.

*　　*　　*

Convolvulus but blooms to die;
A wind-flower suggests a sigh;
Love-lies-bleeding makes me sad;
And poppy-juice would drive me mad:—
But give me holly, bold and jolly,
Honest, prickly, shining holly;
Pluck me holly leaf and berry
For the day when I make merry.

*   *   *

Is the moon tired? she looks so pale
Within her misty veil:
She scales the sky from east to west,
And takes no rest.

Before the coming of the night
The moon shows papery white;
Before the dawning of the day
She fades away.

*   *   *

O Lady Moon, your horns point toward the east;
    Shine, be increased:
O Lady Moon, your horns point toward the west;
    Wane, be at rest.

INDEX: FIRST LINES

INDEX: TITLES